SIKH SAKHIS

FOR THE YOUTH

Canadian Sikh Study & Teaching Society
P.O. Box 60153 Fraser Postal Outlet
6417 Fraser Street, Vancouver, B.C.
Canada V5W 4B5

Canadian Sikh Study & Teaching Society
P.O. Box 60153 Fraser Postal Outlet
6417 Fraser Street, Vancouver, B.C.
Canada V5W 4B5

First Published in 1988 by Satnam Education Society,
Vancouver, B.C.

Second Edition 1989
Revised & Enlarged Fourth Edition 1994

Canadian Cataloguing in Publication Data

Singh, Gurbakhsh, 1927 -
Sikh Sakhies for the Youth

ISBN 0-9694092-6-5

1. Sikhs--Biography--Juvenile literature
2. Sikhism--History--Juvenile literature
    I. Canadian Sikh Study & Teaching Society
    II. Title.
BL2017.8.S56 1994   j294.6'092'2   C94-910075-7

DEDICATED
TO
THE YOUTH

ON WHOSE SHOULDERS LIES THE
RESPONSIBILTY OF ESTABLISHING
EVER LASTING PEACE, TRUTH AND
JUSTICE IN THE WORLD.

PUBLISHER'S NOTE

Born in the village of , Gill Distt. Ludhiana Punjab on September 15th 1927, Dr. Gurbakhsh Singh studied at Lyallpur and Khalsa College, Amritsar. He obtained his Ph. D. degree from Ohio State University U.S.A. in 1963 and served as a Professor and Dean at Panjab Agricultural University Ludhiana.

Dr. Gurbakhsh Singh was also fortunate to be in the company of Sant Teja Singth Mastuana (M.A., LL.B., A.M. Harvard University) for many years, who inspired him to study Sikh religion and preach Sikhism to the youth of North America. He resigned in 1984 and since then he has been very active teaching Sikh religion to our youth.

Professor Singh is a very devoted Gursikh to the cause of Guru Khalsa Panth, and his scholarly lectures on Sikhism have tremendous effect on the minds of youth. Needless to say, Sikh youth love listening to him.

Canadian Sikh Study and Teaching Society is very grateful to Dr. Gurbakhsh Singh for permitting us to publish his works.

iv

ACKNOWLEDGMENTS

First Edition

It is with great pleasure that the author thanks the youth for their cooperation in making this book possible. The positive response given by the youth while listening to these sakhis during Sikh youth camps motivated the author to print them in the form of a booklet for them.

Two youths, Surinder Singh of Vancouver, B.C., Canada, and Gurpreet Singh of McLean, Virginia, U.S.A., were requested to critically read the manuscript. They made very useful suggestions to improve it. The author met S. Ralph Singh at the Sikh Youth Camps and took advantage of his advice to make the book more useful for the youth. Thanks to S. Baljit Singh, of Richmond, B.C., who typed the manuscript.

Thanks also to S.S. Guru Raj Kaur Khalsa and S.S. Hari Singh Khalsa, of Vancouver, B.C., who gave their time to typeset the final copy and prepare it for the printer.

Comments from the readers are welcome to improve this book, which is intended to make the Sikh youth develop deep love for their faith.

Second Edition

The author is thankful to the critical observations of the youth regarding the first edition. After reviewing it, the immediate reaction of the trainees was, "How come the sakhis related to the brave Sikh women are not there?" Accordingly, a new section, *Part III - Brave Sikh Women*, has been added.

Third Edition

More sakhis have been added to meet the need of a reference book for the Sikh youth Gurmat camps. The author is thankful to the Sikh Missionary College, Ludhiana, Punjab, India for the use of booklets published by them.

A ninth grade youth, Balpreet Kaur, Fredericksburg, Va., read the manuscript critically and made many useful changes. The author is obliged to Sardar Santokh Singh, retired principal, Khalsa School, Vancouver, for editing the draft and suggesting valuable additions to it. The translation of the prelude to the Sikh prayer, printed on the inside of the front cover, was kindly edited by Ms. Georgia E. Rangel.

Typing and format sewa was done by Taranjeet Singh Athwal, Richmond, Canada.

Gurbakhsh Singh, Ph.D.
Vancouver, B.C., September 1992

PREFACE

Sikh *sakhis* for the Youth is the result of the interest and response shown by the young trainees at the Sikh Youth Camps during the past five years, to understand their glorious past. During 1987, the participants desired written hand-outs for keeping record of what they were told in the history classes.

Listening to the *sakhis* of the Sikh shaheeds was a great experience for them. Many of them volunteered to narrate those *sakhis* during the morning and evening gatherings in the Gurdwaras. Many words and sentences included in the book were picked up from the speeches made by the youth, because they conveyed the message more effectively in their own language.

An effort was made to represent each *sakhi* as a two-line rhyme. On the suggestions and the experience of the youth in reciting them, the rhymes were modified again and again to make them better and easy to sing. The final version of the rhymes developed in the camps is stated at the beginning of each *sakhi* of the martyrs in Part II of the book.

The *sakhis* related to the life of Guru Nanak Dev were told to the participants during 1986. They form Part I of the book. The youth is requested to read the *sakhis* not just as a story to please him or her, but as a lesson for becoming a better person. Accordingly, at the end of each *sakhi*, the lesson to be learned has been mentioned, and appears in bold italic lettering.

Part III was added when the youth specifically desired to know the *sakhis* regarding the bravery shown by the Sikh women and the sacrifices made by them becoming role models for succeeding generations.

Part IV includes additional *sakhis* told to the trainees during 1990 at the camps.

This book has been revised to be used by both young and senior youths.

CONTENTS

PART I

GURU NANAK SAKHIS

Love God and live truthfully,
Be honest and share your earnings.

1

GURU NANAK DEV

Founder of the Revolution, Sikhism

In 1469 at village Rai Bhoi di, Talwandi, District Sheikhupura, Pakistan (then Punjab, India), a new light came to the world. This light later was called Guru Nanak Dev. The Guru would bring a social and religious revolution. After the name of the Guru, the village later became known as Nankana Sahib.

Guru Nanak felt deep anguish when he observed the followers of one faith hating the followers of other faiths. Among the Hindus, a large section of society was considered low caste or untouchables.

Women were treated as inferior human beings. The Guru described the practice of this inequality among the people as a sin and strongly protested against it. Guru Nanak gave new directions to the divided society to destroy it's caste, creed, and other barriers. His preaching united all people under one category -- as equal human beings. He emphatically told them that being the children of the same Father, God, they were all equals.

To implement his teachings Guru Nanak founded the institutions of *sangat* and *pangat* where people would sit together, pray together, and eat together without any discrimination of caste, color, creed, or faith. Nobody was considered inferior or superior regardless of his birth or wealth.

His teachings included the following major directions to the people:

1) Sincere Love For God, *Nam Japna*. The very idea of one common Father for all humanity, teaches us that whatever name, Allah, Ram, Gobind, Guru, etc., we may use for the Almighty, we all are His creation and therefore must love each other as brothers and sisters.

2) Honest Earnings, *Dharam Di Kirt*. It is only hard earned money which is sweet like honey. Wealth collected through corruption and unfair means makes the mind dirty and evil. Those who become dependent upon other people's earnings, usually become their mental slaves. Such economic dependence limits their independent thinking and speaking.

3) Sharing Earnings, *Wand Ke Chhakna*. Because we are children of the same Father, we should feel pleasure in sharing our earnings with the needy. People who share with the needy do not oblige them or do any favor to them, but are just doing their duty which is expected of them. Sikhs do not give charity or donations to anyone. They share their earnings with them. The only Giver in the world is God. How can we give anything as a donation when we are mere custodians of the gifts given to us by Him?

4) Accepting The Will Of God, *Bhana Mannana*. God knows what is right or wrong for the overall welfare of people. We should accept His decisions without any grudge or question.

5) Goodwill For All, *Sarbat Ka Bhala*. A Sikh is required to pray to God at least twice a day for His blessings. In his prayer, he requests God for the welfare of the whole humanity, not just of his community or his family alone.

Thus, Guru Nanak brought a social and religious

revolution by providing a platform, *sangat* and *pangat*, where all people could pray, meet and eat together as equals without any kind of discrimination. He was, therefore, remembered as a great holy man in the following folk lore: *Nanak Shah Fakir, Hindu ka Guru, Musalman ka Pir.*

Guru Nanak is a selfless saintly sage,
Respected by every religion and every age.

God is the creator of this Universe. We all, whatever our caste, color, creed, country, or faith, have been begotten by Him as His children. Accordingly do not consider any human being as low or inferior. Treat and respect all persons as equals and wish well for everyone.

2

SACHA SAUDA

The True Bargain

Doing good to the people is the way of a Sikh.
Sharing with the needy, makes the day of a Sikh.

(Guru) Nanak used to run a shop in his village, Talwandi, now called Nankana Sahib. When making purchases for his shop, he often went to a nearby town called Chuhar Kana. On the way to the town, there was a resting place where holy people who were passing through the city could stay.

(Guru) Nanak often visited these religious people to have discussions with them regarding God and his blessings. Nanak often shared his earnings with these holy men and needy people. Whenever he had a chance to be in their company, he exchanged views regarding the purpose of human life.

His father, Kalyan Chand, popularly known as Mehta Kalu, did not appreciate (Guru) Nanak Dev's conduct. Kalyan Chand advised Nanak not to lavishly give away money, food, and other articles. But Nanak continued helping people including those who would stop at Chuhar Kana on their pilgrimages. In memory of Nanak's gracious acts Gurdwara, Sacha Sauda stands there reminding us, *God wants us to share our earnings with the needy.*

Finally, the father asked his son to limit his habit of giving charity to the people. Rather, he wanted him to save money for future use. Nanak explained to his father that sharing money with the needy people is the "True Bargain" of life and everyone should adapt it to his ability. It is an essential duty of a human being and the right path for peace and the pleasure of the people. However, the father insisted that (Guru) Nanak should abandon the practice of giving away money and other articles. Nanaki, the elder sister of Nanak, who was married and lived at Sultanpur Lodhi was called to help settle the issue. According to the decision (Guru) Nanak Dev left Talwandi and went with his sister to her town to work there. Guru Nanak was popular with all people. He was known for his competency to manage stores and deal in them. He was therefore given the job of managing the stores of the local government at the new place. It may be mentioned here that during those days, money was rare and most of the dealings were made in kind. Managing government stores was an honorable and a very important assignment for a person.

Let us resolve today, being the followers of Guru Nanak, that we should utilize a part of our earnings for sharing with the people who need our help. This is the true bargain of life

The true bargain of life is sharing one's earning with the needy and helping them in whatever way we can.

3

LIVING HONESTLY

Truth is above everything.
Highest is truthful living.

(Guru) Nanak Dev was a successful shopkeeper in his village, Talwandi. Because of his honesty and integrity, he was appointed manager of the government stores at Sultanpur Lodhi, in Punjab, on the banks of the river Bayeen. This was a job of great responsibility as large stores and stocks were involved in government dealings. One could easily misappropriate lots of money or stores. Junior officials were usually not very sincere. On the contrary, they were quite often dishonest.

All residents of the town were satisfied with the good dealings of (Guru) Nanak Dev. The employees, however, did not like any strict control over them. They were always on the look out for an excuse to complain against him. (Guru) Nanak often gave a lot of money and food to the needy people. Whenever any person needed support, (Guru) Nanak was always ready to help him. The corrupt employees did not like the honest conduct of Nanak. Tired of him, they alleged that Nanak was giving away government stocks to make a good name for himself. The people knew about the greatness of Nanak and, therefore, refused to believe these rumors.

Finally, the employees lodged a complaint with the Nawab that (Guru) Nanak Dev was mis-appropriating stores and stocks. Continued complaints regarding mishandling of the stores forced the

Nawab to check the accounts, and stores. To the great embarrassment of the Nawab, everything was in order. There was no shortage at all, as doubted by the authorities. Most employees, who themselves were corrupt and had complained to defame (Guru) Nanak, felt very ashamed.

Even after this incident, the employees did not mend their ways. They kept spreading rumors against the "Guru." They became even more jealous because of his rising popularity. Therefore, after some time, they again raised the same issue and started telling people that (Guru) Nanak was not keeping the accounts properly. The second inspection of stores proved once more that all complaints by the employees were false and malicious. The evil intentions of the employees became known to everyone. All the residents of the village appreciated the honest living of (Guru) Nanak and the sharing of his earnings with other people. Even the Nawab of the town respected him as a holy man.

After demonstrating the principles of truthful living, he decided to deliver this message to the people of the world. To achieve his mission, he made plans to go on long tours. (Guru) Nanak Dev resigned his job even though the Nawab repeatedly requested him to stay there.

A Sikh earns his living honestly. Dishonest earnings are unpious, hence are prohibited to a Sikh in the same way as eating of beef is prohibited to a Hindu and pork to a Muslim.

4

NEITHER A HINDU NOR A MUSLIM

God is our Father, His children are we.
Love every person and pray to Thee.

(Guru) Nanak Dev, when he was about 30 years old and staying at Sultanpur Lodhi, Punjab, went as usual to a nearby river for bathing. When he did not return for three days the people got very worried and feared he had drowned. They were, however, overjoyed when they saw (Guru) Nanak Dev alive and coming to the village. A big crowd gathered around him. (Guru) Nanak Dev gave his first formal sermon on that day. "God loves everyone of us; for Him there is no Hindu, no Muslim; all of us are his children, hence, equal human beings."

Both Hindus and Muslims loved Nanak and had gathered there to welcome him. He made them all sit together as equals and named the unique congregation *sangat*. The Guru explained his philosophy by reminding them that people are composed of two things: the "body" which in itself is a dead matter and the "life" which makes all actions of the body possible. Ram and Allah are the cause of these two. We are living because the "body" and "life" are together. Then how can we separate Ram and Allah? God, the Almighty, is both Ram and Allah; those who love Him as Ram are called Hindus and those who love Him as Allah are called Muslims. We should remember the truth -- both Hindus and Muslims are human beings created by God and have to be considered as equals.

Guru Nanak Dev while traveling in the Middle East visited Mecca, Baghdad and Madina, the holy places of the Muslims. During his discussions with the Muslim theologians, he was asked who he was. The reply of the Guru was the same, "Neither a Hindu, nor a Muslim, just a human being." They questioned the Guru, as to who was the superior of the two, the one who followed Islam or the one who followed Hinduism. The reply given by the Guru is well documented by Bhai Gurdas, who scribed the first compilation of Adi Guru Granth Sahib. Guru Nanak Dev told them, "Without good deeds, both will repent."

The brave reply of the Guru embarrassed the Muslim religious leaders because they had been preaching that if a person becomes a Muslim, he is assured of reaching heaven after death. The Guru emphasized that God values our deeds and not our beliefs.

All humans, being God's children, have equal status. Sincere honest deeds done to serve human beings are the right path to realize God.

NOTE: This preaching of Nanak has now been accepted by the World Conference for Religions and Peace." According to their declaration at New Jersey, 1979. "Too often the names and practices of our religions have been associated with warfare and strife. Now we must reverse this by: (a) Breaking down barriers of prejudice and hostility between religious communities and institutions. (b) Confronting the powers of the world with the teachings of our religions rather than conforming to them when they act contrary to the well-being of humanity. (c) Building inter religious understanding in our local communities, particularly where prejudices run strong.

5

BHAI LALO

AND

MALIK BHAGO

Taking the rights of others pollutes the mind.
Always be honest, ever be kind.

Guru Nanak Dev stayed with Bhai Lalo when he began his preaching missions. Bhai Lalo was a carpenter who earned his living honestly by working hard all day. The local village official was a corrupt person. He was known as Malik Bhago. One day he invited every resident of the village to a feast, so he could make a good image with the people. Guru Nanak Dev declined to go to the feast. Special messengers were sent to bring him. Bhago offered delicious food to the Guru and in response to his offer, waited for good words from him. Guru Nanak Dev rather than blessing Malik Bhago declined to accept any food from him. Bhago was surprised to hear a refusal for the delicious food and he immediately asked the reason for the refusal.

The Guru told him that the food which Malik Bhago considered to be tasty and sweet was, in fact, made from the blood of the poor. Malik Bhago had been extracting money from the people, instead of living on his honest earnings. Bhago was very much embarrassed by the bold and frank comments of the Guru.

Everyone else appreciated the truth fearlessly spoken by Guru Nanak Dev. Bhago could not deny the allegations made against him at his face in the presence of the respectable people of the village. Good senses prevailed and Malik Bhago confessed his guilt. He requested to be pardoned for his past deeds and promised to live a true and honest life in the future.

Guru Nanak Dev told the gathering there that only honestly earned food, as that of Bhai Lalo, tastes good and sweet like milk. All dishonest earnings are the blood of the innocent. If drops of blood fall on a cloth, it becomes dirty. How can the mind of a person who lives on the blood of the helpless people, remain pious and clean?

Such was the effect of Guru Nanak's piety and personality that people did visualize blood in Malik's delicious dinner and milk in Bhai Lalo's frugal meal.

Taking away the rights of others is like drawing their blood, it pollutes the mind. Honest earnings are like sweet milk, they make the mind pious.

6

SAJJAN THUG

Neither be a robber, nor be a cheat.
Be sincere to all, your dealings be neat.

Sajjan means a nice person, a friend, a helper. There was a man with this name living in Tulamba (now in Pakistan). He was known as a good man in his area. He had constructed an inn for travelers to rest for the night. Whenever a traveler would forget anything in the inn, Sajjan kept it as his own. Slowly he developed the bad habit of stealing valuables of the travelers when they were sleeping at night. After some time, this bad habit made him a wicked man. He even killed people staying at his inn if he wanted to take away the travelers' belongings. The dead bodies were disposed of secretly by burying them in the compound at night. A "sajjan" because of his bad habits thus became a "thug." The people, therefore, called him "Sajjan Thug."

On one of their journeys Guru Nanak Dev and Bhai Mardana stayed with Sajjan Thug for the night. In the evening Guru Nanak Dev sang a shabad while Bhai Mardana played on the rebeck. The shabad explained that if a person is bad at heart, an outward show of good acts means nothing. God knows our mind and no one can bluff Him. The true friends (sajjan) are actually the good deeds of a man. These good deeds help the man not only here in this world but also after death in the next life. By evil acts man makes his own mind dirty, because of which he not only suffers here in this world, but also his soul remains dirty even after death.

Sajjan Thug had been listening to this shabad attentively. As the shabad went into his ears, his mind started "seeing" the truth. He realized he was an evil man. He was taking away the belongings of innocent travelers to whom he was supposed to provide comfort and service.

Sajjan Thug went to the Guru, folded his hands and confessed before the Guru that he was Sajjan only by name. Actually, by his deeds he was a Thug. Sajjan Thug sincerely repented and promised to lead a holy life in the future.

The Guru was pleased by the change of his heart and he was, therefore, very kind to Sajjan Thug. Sajjan was advised to distribute all the ill-got money to the needy and start his life afresh as an honest man. He sincerely practised as the Guru advised him. He started helping the visitors and making their stay comfortable by whatever he could do for them.

Thus, a Sajjan by name, a thug by profession, became a Sajjan by his deeds as well, after meeting Guru Nanak.

Man is valued by the deeds he does. True friends are our good deeds. They remain with us even when our body dies.

7

HOLLOW RITUALS HAVE NO VALUE

Service to people is service to God
Rituals, if hollow, value not.

Guru Nanak Dev while on his eastward journey reached Hardwar. It is on the banks of the river Ganges and is one of the major centers for Hindu pilgrimage. The people, gathered there in large numbers, were bathing in the holy river. Guru Nanak Dev observed many people throwing water towards the sun in the east. The Guru had already heard about this meaningless ritual. He, therefore, thought it the right place and the proper time to give correct guidance that those kinds of mindless hollow rituals have no value.

Guru Nanak Dev entered the river for purposes of bathing as other common pilgrims were doing. Instead of throwing water to the east, he, however, started throwing water in the opposite direction towards the west. Taking him as a naive visitor, the nearby bathers told him that he was not performing the rituals correctly. They advised him to throw water to the east. Guru Nanak Dev continued throwing water towards the west pretending that he was very much absorbed in the 'holy' act and had not heard anything. Soon, many people gathered there to tell him that the proper method of performing the ritual was to throw water in the other direction. His water thrown to the west was of no use to him or to his dead ancestors.

Seeing a lot of people around, Guru Nanak stopped throwing water, looked towards them and asked, "What is the matter? What is wrong with my throwing water?" Many people spoke in one voice. "The water is to be thrown towards the rising sun so that it reaches your dead ancestors." Guru Nanak Dev replied that his crops in his village were dying. The village is toward the west. He wanted to irrigate those crops. After hearing this reply the people started laughing. One of them questioned him as to how the water thrown by him could reach hundreds of miles away. The Guru became serious and asked, "If the water thrown by me cannot reach a few hundred miles away on this very earth, how can water thrown by you to your dead ancestors reach them in the heavens?"

The people became silent and started thinking over the reply given by the Guru. They had no logical argument to challenge his statement.

Guru Nanak Dev came out of the river and the crowd followed him. The Guru calmly told them the truth. He explained that hollow rituals do not have any religious value. They should love, respect and take care of their parents when they are alive. When people die, they do not need anything from us and neither can we send them anything after they have left this world. After death, people get what they had given to the needy, out of their honest earnings, while living on this earth.

Serve your parents and others when they are alive. Hollow, mindless rituals after their death, have no value to them at all.

8

TRUTH

AND

FALSEHOOD

Life is merely a temporary charm.
Be good to all and do no harm.

Guru Nanak Dev reached Sialkot, now in Pakistan, on one of his preaching missions. The people, who came to see him, told him that they were greatly worried about themselves and their city. The Guru asked the reason for that. They said that a Muslim mystic named Hamza Gaus had gone on a 40-day meditation to destroy the city and its residents. This was because he was angry with the behavior of one person. He made a decision to use his powers to make the whole city sink into the earth and make it vanish forever. Guru Nanak Dev assured them that no harm would come to them. They should go and get busy with their jobs and always keep God in their mind.

The Guru went to the place where the Pir had locked himself in a chamber in which he sat meditating to destroy the city. Bhai Mardana was asked to play on the rebeck while the Guru started singing a shabad. The Pir heard the music and virtues of God sung outside his chamber. He broke his 40-day continuous meditation, opened the door and came out. He was surprised to see the Guru

17

and his associates. He asked them, "Who are you? Why have you come here and interrupted my meditation?"

The Guru told him to calm down and reminded him that holy men are expected to serve and help the people with the power and virtues God bestows on them. It is a sin to use the holy powers to harm people. Pir insisted that all the people of the city were evil. None possessed any goodness. They all deserved to be destroyed. The Guru decided to reveal the truth to him. He gave some money to his associate and sent him to the city to purchase a packet each of "truth" and "falsehood."

The person went to the city and moved from shop to shop in search of truth and falsehood. He always got a negative answer to his query. Finally, he contacted Bhai Moola. He took the money and wrote on a piece of paper, Marna Sach, Jeona Jhuth. "Death is a truth and life is a falsehood."

The Guru showed this to the Pir and warned him that he was totally wrong to think of doing any harm to such people. There were people who knew and understood that life is temporary, hence, a falsehood. Death is sure to come to everyone. While after death, our soul lives forever hence, death is a truth.

Pir confessed that he was wrong to believe that everybody was bad and needed to be destroyed. He decided to serve the people and not harm them with the knowledge and virtues that God had given him.

Powers given by God should be used to help people and not harm them. Life is a temporary phase, death is inevitable.

PART II

SIKH MARTYRS

Fear None, Frighten None
Love the Lord, Mighty One

PRELUDE

Guru Nanak Dev, born in 1469, was a religious and social revolutionary. He protested against the injustice done to the people by both the political rulers and the religious authorities of the time.

The ruling community, the Muslims, came from the Middle East. Being all powerful, they considered themselves superior human beings and denied the social rights to their Hindu subjects. They wanted the Hindus to become Muslims and used force to achieve this aim. They often tortured them and even killed them for refusing to give up their faith. Brahmans, the priestly class, too, sucked the blood of the poor Hindu masses. They had the sole right to perform social and religious functions and therefore were able to extract forced donations from them. To refuse the helpless people their social and religious rights, the Brahmans cooperated with the ruling Muslims. About a fifth of the local Indian people were degraded as low-caste, untouchables and treated even worse than animals.

Because of these pressures, many Hindus became Muslims. Low caste people adopted Islam to wash the stigma of being considered low grade human beings.

The Brahmans assumed the status of the highest class. According to them, the Khatris, the fighting class, were next, while the working majority, Vaish, farmers and traders, were given the third rank in society. Women were considered "incomplete" and "unclean" persons and were not entitled to the same status as men.

To educate people regarding their human rights and Sikh philosophy, Guru Nanak founded the institutions of *sangat* and *pangat*, where all people would sit together as equals without any kind of discrimination on the basis of birth, worth, sex, creed, color, etc. When they joined together to sing praises of the Lord, their congregation was called *sangat* and when they sat together to eat *langar*, they were called *pangat*. To obtain solace, all people, Hindus and Muslims irrespective of their caste, flocked to join *sangat* and *pangat*. The idea of providing equal rights to all human beings was a revolutionary concept.

This organized movement which rejected the oppression of the people, through political, social or religious authority, was not to the liking of the rulers or the Hindu religious leaders. They wanted to destroy this movement and for that purpose they adopted all possible means within their power. The Gurus fearlessly continued to preach against the social and religious evils and protested against the repressive policy of the state. When the state adopted violent methods to finish this movement of religious and human rights, the Sikhs were forced to defend themselves with the sword.

Guru Amar Das was charged with defiling the Hindu faith because he permitted everyone including the untouchables to take water from the same baoli (open well with steps reaching the water level) and letting everyone sit together as equals in the *pangat*. The Guru was summoned to the court. Akbar, the then emperor of Delhi, listened to both sides and rejected the memorandum of the people who complained against the Guru. Later, during the rule of Jehangir who had decided to check the wave of Sikhism, Guru Arjan Dev was arrested, taken to Lahore, and tortured to death in 1606. Instead of being demoralized or terrorized because of this violence as intended by the rulers, the Sikhs exhibited great bravery and fearlessness. They repulsed all four attacks of the Emperor's army during the life of Guru Har Gobind, the son of Guru Arjan Dev.

The harassment of the Gurus continued far into the seventeenth and eighteenth centuries. Guru Teg Bahadur, the ninth Guru and his three associates Bhai Mati Das, Bhai Sati Das, Bhai Dyala were tortured and brutally killed. Guru Gobind Singh was also attacked many times and forced to leave Anandpur, of course, after being assured of peace. Breaking their oaths, the joint army of the Hindu rajas and the Emperor of Delhi attacked the Sikhs when they were out of the fort. Thousands of Sikhs and all four sons of the Guru were killed. The older two gave their lives at Chamkaur defending religious freedom and human rights, while the younger two were murdered by the Nawab of Sirhind. The Sikhs defeated the Imperial army at Mukatsar in the last battle after which the Guru established a new Sikh center at Talwandi, District Bhatinda. The Gurdwara there is now known as Takhat Damdama Sahib.

After the death of Guru Gobind Singh in 1708 at Nanded, Maharashtra, the Sikhs continued their struggle against state repression, first, under the guidance of Baba Gurbakhsh Singh, popular as Banda Singh Bahadur, up to 1716 and then under other Sikh leaders chosen after his death. The people finally obtained full freedom from all kinds of state and religious terrorism. Hindus and Muslims jointly ruled Punjab under the leadership of Maharaja Ranjit Singh.

The *sakhis* of some Sikh martyrs of this period are mentioned in this book to tell how bravely they faced state terrorism, and shed their blood to protect religious freedom and human rights.

1

MARTYRDOM OF

BABA AJIT SINGH
and
BABA JUJHAR SINGH

Sawa lakh se ek laraoon
Tabe Gobind Singh Nam Kahaoon

Truth is stronger than a gun.
Millions can be defeated by one.

With the objective of killing or capturing Guru Gobind Singh, the joint forces of the emperor of Delhi and the rajas of Himachal Pardesh attacked Anandpur Sahib. They encircled the town, and did not allow any food to be taken inside, in the hope of starving the Guru and his followers out. They lost thousands of men while attacking the Guru who was occupying the forts. Having failed to defeat the Guru, they promised him, on solemn oath, a safe passage if he voluntarily left the place. They further assured him that later on, he could come back again to Anandpur as and when he desired. The army generals hoped to give the emperor an image of their victory if they could make the Guru leave Anandpur Sahib.

When the Guru left the fort, the generals broke their oath and the army attacked him with all their might. To make conditions worse for the Sikhs, the nearby river Sirsa was in flood. While fighting and crossing the river, many Sikh lives were lost and those who could cross the river were dispersed. Guru Gobind Singh with his two elder sons and only 40 Sikhs reached a nearby village called Chamkaur where they occupied a mud house called garhi, a mini fort.

The pursuing forces in great numbers tented around it and challenged the Guru that he would not be allowed to leave alive. With the hope of arresting the Guru they attacked the Garhi. The Guru would send a small band of Sikhs to go out and fight the enemy to keep them away from the gate of the Garhi and not let them enter it. The Guru himself sat at the top shooting arrows to check the attacking columns of soldiers. One of the army generals lost his life while attempting to get near the Guru to kill him. The fast arrow shot by the Guru hit the general in the chest, and brought him down from his horse, killing him then and there. This struck fear in the army, which quickly retreated. Afterwards, they moved forward very cautiously and slowly towards the Garhi.

When the fighting was at its height, Baba Ajit Singh, the eldest son of the Guru, then only 18 years of age requested that his father let him join the defending *jatha*. The Guru gladly agreed to permit him to fight the army to keep them away from the Garhi. Having been blessed by his father, Baba Ajit Singh armed himself and went outside the Garhi along with other Sikhs. He fought bravely and fearlessly. He exhibited great fighting skills which surprised the enemy soldiers. The Guru saw all that with his own eyes, and was very satisfied at the bravery of his son. Finally, Baba Ajit Singh fell in the battlefield and thus attained martyrdom.

His younger brother, Jujhar Singh was also watching him fight on the battleground and decided to follow the lead of his brother. He went to his father and expressed his desire to go out with the next *jatha* and continue the struggle to blunt the sword of state terrorism. Though only 14 years old, he was permitted by his father to sacrifice his life to protect the principles of the Sikh faith. Along with other Sikhs, Baba Jujhar Singh put up a good defense like an experienced soldier, as he had obtained a thorough training at Anandpur Sahib. The Guru was very much satisfied with his fighting skill. Having resisted the wave of the enemy soldiers, for a long time, he followed his elder brother and became a martyr.

The Guru thanked the Almighty, that his children attained martyrdom before his own eyes. They gave their lives so that other children could live in peace and freedom from oppression by the state.

The resistance offered by the fearless and brave Sikhs, was so great that the soldiers could not enter the Garhi during the day-long fighting. At night the Guru along with three Sikhs left the Garhi and passed safely through the army camps to finally defeat the army at Mukatsar five months after that.

This unique and great sacrifice by the sons of the Guru would be remembered forever by the people who respect human rights and freedom to worship.

When all other efforts fail, it is justified to take a sword and protect your life and right of worship.

NOTE: The Guru along with the two pyaras, Bhai Daya Singh and Bhai Dharam Singh left the garhi at night, leaving Bhai sangat Singh and a few other Sikhs behind. They were told to keep the army engaged the next day when the fighting restarts. In the morning when the army attacked the Sikhs they were ready to defend themselves. Finally, when all Sikhs fell fighting the soldiers entered the Garhi. The commanders were overjoyed to see the dead body of sangat Singh because they mistook him for the Guru. Later, when more people were shown the dead body, they identified it not to be that of Guru Gobind Singh. The commanders felt ashamed of their failure to kill or capture the Guru. This is how they learned the lesson that truth is stronger than a gun, and millions can be defeated by one.

2

MARTYRDOM OF

BABA ZORAWAR SINGH
and
BABA FATEH SINGH

Why lose your faith to save your life,
Faith lives with you, even after you die.

The joint forces of the emperor and the rajas of the Himachal, not considering their solemn promises given to the tenth Guru, attacked him when he left the fort of Anandpur Sahib. It was a cold winter night of December, 1704. Attack by the enemy forces and difficulties of crossing the flooded Sirsa river resulted in the separation of the Sikhs. As mentioned in the previous *sakhi*, Guru Gobind Singh with his two elder sons and forty Sikhs reached the village Chamkaur. The two younger sons of the Guru and his mother were lost and reached the village of Kheri. They went to the house of Gangu, who used to serve them at Anandpur. To obtain awards from the government for helping them arrest the children and the mother of the Guru, Gangu reported the matter to the police stationed at Morinda. The policemen quickly came to Gangu's house, arrested them and took them to the Governor of Sirhind, to obtain rewards for catching the "rebels".

What greater catch could the governor dream of than capturing alive the family of the Guru, particularly because he had failed to kill the Guru? He decided to convert the young sons of the Guru to Islam by any means. He offered many baits to the children and made promises of royal life if they agreed to become Muslims. The boys, however, remained firm in their faith. Therefore, the governor adapted the force and a harsh attitude to pressure them into becoming Muslims.

To torture them, the children and their grandmother were locked up in a watchtower, which was very cold. They sat all night without even a blanket to put around them. The elder son, Baba Zorawar Singh was just 8 years old, while the younger son, Baba Fateh Singh was only 6 years old.

The children exhibited no fear at all when they were presented the next day, in the court of Wazid Khan, the governor. They acted gracefully like princes and with great self confidence uttered, Waheguru Ji Ka Khalsa, Waheguru Ji Ki Fateh. This angered Wazid Khan very much. He was annoyed that the children had not bowed before him, to show him respect. He personally threatened them with many forms of punishment and torture if they did not act according to his wishes and embrace Islam. The children again firmly refused to give up their faith.

Having failed to frighten the children and mold them to his wishes, Wazid felt humiliated. When Baba Zorawar Singh and Fateh Singh bluntly told him they would not adopt Islam under the threats of death or torture, he ordered them to be bricked alive in a wall.

While being bricked, the children showed no sign of fear or sadness on their faces. When asked to save their lives by giving up their faith, they again firmly said, "No!" When the wall reached their shoulders, it is said it fell down. The children were taken out from the debris and were heartlessly murdered in cold blood.

This sacrifice of Guru Gobind Singh's sons, only six and eight years old, will forever be remembered by young and old alike to learn lessons from their lives. Firm belief in faith, freedom of worship, and refusal to submit to any kind of attack by rulers is the way to live or to die.

Retaining his faith for a Sikh, is superior to retaining his life. Whatever we may do, inevitably we are going to die. Why not die with courage?

Note: These kinds of tyrannical acts of the rulers revealed imbalance of their mind and their unsuitability to run the government. The people were enraged and revolted against them. When Banda Singh Bahadur came to Punjab, the people attacked Sirhind in 1710, destroying all roots of the oppressive rule.

3

KAKA HAKIKAT RAI

Sikhs do not lie, even if they have to die.

The people of Punjab, both Hindus and Muslims, rose against the terrorist rule of Nawab (Governor) Sirhind. The Nawab was killed in 1710, i.e., just half a decade after he murdered the two innocent sons of Guru Gobind Singh. This brought a rule of peace and justice in the area of Punjab, east of Amritsar.

To again take over the control of Punjab from Banda, a strong army was sent from Delhi. The army generals feared to fight a battle with Banda, hence they tricked him with the pretension of having a dialogue with him for peace. They unarmed him and arrested him. His 700 men were also made prisoners along with a teenage boy, Hakikat Rai. All of them were taken to Delhi and asked to surrender to the Emperor. They refused bluntly. The government ordered the murder of everyone. About 100 Sikhs were murdered every day near Chandni Chauk Delhi.

The mother of Hakikat Rai, whose only support and hope of life was her son, submitted a petition to the government to save the life of the boy. She narrated that her son was not a Sikh but was there in the Sikh camp when he was arrested. The Emperor ordered the release of the boy if the boy himself denied being a Sikh. The mother dashed with the release orders, to the place where the Sikhs were murdered. Her son was still waiting for his turn to be killed. Presenting the Farman -- the order of the emperor -- to the Kazi

(Judge) supervising the murdering of the Sikhs, she requested the release of her son.

The Kazi called Hakikat Rai and asked him if he was a Sikh. The boy replied that he certainly was a Sikh. His mother intervened and told the Kazi that the boy was her son and she knew that he was not a Sikh. The boy emphasized that he was a committed Sikh. The son and the mother started arguing with each other. Khafi Khan, a Muslim historian, an eye witness who recorded these horrifying killings, was very surprised to hear those arguments.

The mother again asserted that her son was not a Sikh. However, the boy raising his voice retorted immediately that his mother was telling a lie in order to save his life. His father was dead, and he was the only support for her. Being a Sikh, he wanted to be murdered without further delay so that he may not be left behind by his Sikh associates already murdered. Before another word could be said by his mother, the boy was standing with his head bent before the butcher. The sword in the hand of the butcher lowered and Hakikat Rai attained his martyrdom.

Such blood curdling events of Sikh history made Sikhs stronger and even more fearless of the oppression let loose against them. Even today Sikhs don't hesitate to die for justice and human rights.

Even under a threat to their life, Sikhs do not tell a lie. They love to live as Sikhs or, they would prefer to die.

4

SHAHEED

BABA BANDA SINGH BAHADUR

Many places in Delhi are there to tell,
Sikhs love their faith, at no cost do they sell.

Baba Banda Singh was born in 1670. He was named Lachhman Das. His parents lived in Rajauri, a village in Jammu region, to the north of Punjab. He left Jammu and wandered in search of peace. After years of wandering, he reached Nanded, a small town on the banks of Godawari, a famous sacred river of south India. He established his 'dera' near the city. Then he was called Madho Das Bairagi, because of his detachment from family life.

When he went to the south, in 1708, Guru Gobind Singh camped in Nanded. One day, when the Guru happened to go to the "dera", the Bairagi tried his many tricks and magic to impress the Guru, but failed. He soon realized that the visitor to his 'dera' was no ordinary person, but a great master. He fell to the feet of the Guru and felt solace in his mind. When the Guru asked him who he was, he answered, "Master, this is your Banda (slave)."

The Guru was pleased with Bairagi's character, and gave him Khanda-Bata-Pahaul, thus renaming him Gurbakhsh Singh, but the humbly said words "Your Banda" remained stuck to him, giving him the popular name Banda Bahadur. Because of his great qualities, Banda Bahadur was made the leader of the Khalsa and sent to the Punjab to destroy the roots of the evil rule of the Nawab of Sirhind. Five other Singhs were sent with Banda Bahadur as his advisors.

When the people in the Punjab came to know of his arrival, they rallied around him and offered him all kinds of help. The masses revolted against the tyrannical government and sided with Banda to dislodge the rulers. The important cities of Samana, Banur, etc. fell quickly to the armies of the people. Finally, Sirhind was taken in 1710. The governor who had murdered the two innocent sons and the mother of the Guru there in 1704, was killed.

Banda started a rule of peace and justice. However, when Farkhseer became the Emperor, he sent a strong army to capture Banda. In 1716, Banda was surrounded from all sides but still the army would not dare to face him. According to a Muslim author, Mohd Qusim, "Such was the terror of the Sikhs and the fear of the sorcery of the Sikh chief that the commander of the army prayed that God might so ordain things that Banda should seek safety in his flight from the fortress."

Banda was tricked and caught by the commander pretending that the Emperor was willing to have a dialogue and settle with him by making him the king of Jammu, his home state. After his arrest, Banda along with his 700 men, was taken to Delhi.

All efforts by the Emperor to convert Banda or any of his men to Islam, failed. The frustrated Emperor ordered the cruel method of killing them all, i.e., by cutting off the head of every Sikh in public. About 100 Sikhs were murdered daily near Chandni Chauk. Finally Banda was brutally tortured and killed.

Before his murder, one Mughal noble interviewed Banda and stated, "It is surprising that one who shows so much nobility should have been guilty of such horrors." Banda replied, "Whenever men become so corrupt and wicked so as to relinquish the path of equity and abandon themselves to all kinds of excesses, then providence never fails to raise up a scourge like me to chastise a race so depraved, but when the measure of punishment is full, then he raises up men like you to bring him to punishment."

Corrupt and wicked rulers are punished by saint-soldiers deputed by God.

5

SHAHEEDS

BHAI SUBEG SINGH

and

BHAI SHAHBAJ SINGH

Khalsa willingly make sacrifice.
People may have peace all their life.

Bhai Subeg Singh was a person of high character, and a great scholar of the Persian language. He lived near Lahore and worked as a contractor. For some time he accepted the job of the Kotwal, the sheriff of Lahore. Because of his good administrative skills, not only the people, but Zakaria Khan, the governor of Lahore, also respected him very much. Khalsa Panth, as well, held Bhai Subeg Singh in great esteem because he lived like a true Sikh and always helped the Khalsa.

Having failed to subdue the Khalsa through violence and terrorism, Zakaria decided to befriend them. He thought of living in peace with Sikhs by giving up all oppression against them. With that purpose in mind, he offered a deal to the Khalsa which said:

1) The government will allot a Jagir to the Khalsa and honor their leader with the title of "Nawab" and present to him a valuable formal robe worn by the

kings;

2) In response to this gesture of good will, the Khalsa will cooperate with the government and not oppose or defy their rule.

Bhai Subeg Singh was requested by the Nawab (governor) of Lahore to use his good offices with the Sikhs, and settle the deal. When the offer was presented before the Khalsa, staying in the forests, they declined it. On the request of Bhai Subeg Singh not to waste that chance for peaceful life in villages, the Khalsa accepted it. S. Kapoor Singh was asked by the Khalsa to accept the robe and the title. He has since been known as Nawab Kapoor Singh.

Shahbaj Singh, son of Bhai Subeg Singh, was 18 years old and studying Persian under the guidance of a Kazi, i.e., a Muslim theologian, a judge. The Kazi was very much impressed by the intellectual level, unique physical beauty and very good behavior of the Sikh youth. He wanted a person like him to be a Muslim rather than a *kafir* (non-believer) as the non-Muslims were called then. The Kazi started preaching Islam to Subeg Singh and assured him many privileges if he became a Muslim. However, the Sikh youth remained firmly stuck to his beliefs. He had studied that Sikhism teaches love and respect for every human being. He argued that there was no reason for him to become a Muslim and to restrict his thought to one community alone.

Having failed to motivate the boy to adopt Islam, the Kazi threatened him with severe tortures if he continued to express his firm dedication to Sikhism. The Kazi soon lost his patience and decided to forcibly convert both the father and the son to his faith.

A false case was registered with the Lahore police in 1733 that both, the son as well as the father, had used disrespectful words for Mohammed, the prophet of Islam. Without making any inquiry and forgetting their good character and the service rendered to the government in bringing about reconciliation with the Sikhs, Zakaria ordered their arrest and torture. All possible methods were adopted to frighten and torture them to break their will. However, both the Sikhs stood fast and stuck to their faith. The Nawab ordered their murder by a very cruel way, i.e., crushing them in between two rotating sharp toothed wheels (charkharhi).

The Sikhs lost their lives, but not their faith. It is the faith which is everlasting and not the life.

Why lose your faith, which is going to be with you forever, for the sake of a few more days on this earth, which everyone has to leave anyway.

6

SHAHEED BHAI MANI SINGH

A King can take away the life of a Sikh,
but not his faith or right for worship.

Bhai Mani Singh was a great personality of the 18th century. He is well known for his bravery and scholarship.

Bhai Mani Singh was born in 1644 to Bhai Mai Das. At the age of thirteen, his father took him to Guru Har Rai at Kiratpur from which point on Bhai Mani Singh remained in the service of the Gurus and the Sikh community.

At Anandpur, Bhai Mani Singh transcribed many copies of the sacred Sikh scriptures to send them to different preaching centers in India. He would also teach the reading of gurbani and its philosophy to the Sikhs.

Bhai Mani Singh accompanied Guru Gobind Singh when he went to Paonta, in Himachal, on the banks of the Jamna River. Bhai Mani Singh fought bravely in the Bhangani battle of 1686 to defend Paonta from the joint attack of all the hill rajas. Guru Gobind Singh, after winning the battle returned to Anandpur where the same rajas in 1687 requested him to protect them from the attack of the Army Commander of Kashmir. The Guru agreed to help them. A fierce battle took place at Nadaun in which Bhai Mani Singh took active part in defeating the invader.

During 1704 Anandpur was surrounded by the combined forces of the hill rajas and those of the emperor of Delhi. When the Guru

38

left the city in December, 1704, Bhai Mani Singh was to escort Mata Sunder Kaur and Mata Sahib Kaur to Delhi. He came with them to Takhat Damdama Sahib Talwandi Sabo, where the Guru settled after defeating the Mughal army in the last battle fought at Mukatsar. At Damdama Sahib, Guru Gobind Singh edited the current version of the Guru Granth Sahib. The honor of transcribing it was given to Bhai Mani Singh.

After the death of Banda Singh Bahadur in 1716, unfortunately, the Sikhs were split into factions, Bandai Sikh and Tat (True) Khalsa. Both sides wanted to take control of Amritsar, and thus there was a great likelihood of a mutual fight among the Sikhs. Fortunately, Bhai Mani Singh was able to tactfully reconcile the two factions.

As in charge of the Golden Temple management, Bhai Mani Singh used to call two general gatherings of the Sikhs there, one at Diwali and the other at Baisakhi. This built the morale of the Khalsa and gave them great strength.

In 1738, Zakaria Khan, Governor of Lahore, gave permission for the Diwali gathering only if the Sikhs paid a tax of Rs. 5000. Bhai Mani Singh hoped to collect the money from the Khalsa when they would come to attend the gathering. But the Governor had a different plan. He sent secret orders to his forces to make a surprise attack on the Sikhs during the night of the Baisakhi function. Bhai Mani Singh came to know of this plan, and sent messages to the Sikhs not to come to Amritsar. The Sikhs who did come, had to leave because of the expected attack by the army. Thus, no money could be collected or paid to the government.

Bhai Sahib sent a strong protest to the authorities. They, instead of submitting an apology for their treacherous act, arrested him and took him to Lahore. Bhai Mani Singh showed his inability to pay the money and refused to give up his faith in favor of Islam. He was, therefore, ordered to be killed by cutting his body at each joint. Bhai Mani Singh, who was then 94 years old, thus offered his life struggling for human rights.

It may be mentioned that Bhai Dayala who attained martyrdom at Delhi along with Guru Tegh Bahadur, was the real brother of Bhai Mani Singh.

Bhai Bachittar Singh who turned back the drunken elephant at Anandpur was his son. Bhai Udey Singh, his other son, killed Raja Kesri Chand who brought a big army to attack Anandpur. Eleven brothers and seven out of ten sons of Bhai Mani Singh attained martyrdom for protecting the Truth. His grandfather offered his life fighting Mughal forces during the first battle of Guru Har Gobind to defend Amritsar from the Mughal army. Bhai Mani Singh belongs to a family of great martyrs.

   1) **Khalsa settles its disputes amicably and not by fighting.**

   2) **State can take away the life of Sikhs (saint soldiers) but cannot stop their voice for human rights and freedom of worship.**

SHAHEEDS

BABA GARJA SINGH

and

BABA BOTA SINGH

Khalsa will remain ever alive
Oppression they will always fight.

The first half of the eighteenth century was very harsh for the Sikhs. They made unparalleled sacrifices during this period. The Mughal government decided to finish the very name of the Sikhs from the Punjab, the land of their birth. There was legal permission to loot and rob the house of any Sikh. Rather, handsome cash awards were given for killing a Sikh or getting him caught. This forced the Sikhs to leave their homes and pass their days in inaccessible places, i.e., hills in the north, deserts in the south or the bushes along the rivers.

In their daily prayer, the Sikhs requested Akal Purakh to grant them the gift of *Amritsar de darshan ashnan*. For this they would visit the Golden Temple during night or other odd hours to bathe in the sarovar. While making such attempts many Sikhs were killed by the government forces guarding the approaches to the Golden Temple. The Sikhs did not move about openly in the villages lest the police know about their presence.

Taking advantage of the migration of the Sikhs to secret places, Zakria Khan, Governor of Punjab, announced in all the villages that Sikhs were extinct in Punjab. The government thought this would break the will of the Sikhs and would also discourage people from taking Amrit and joining the wave of the Khalsa Panth.

It was in 1739 that two Sikhs, Baba Garja Singh and Baba Bota Singh, while going to Amritsar were hiding in the bushes along the Taran-Taran-Amritsar Road. During those days the Sikhs used to travel at night and hide during the day. Two travelers passing on that road saw them from a distance. One said to the other, "They appear to be Sikhs." The other replied, "I think you are mistaken. They cannot be Sikhs. Didn't you hear the announcement, made with the beat of the drum, that all Sikhs have been killed."

Baba Garja Singh and Baba Bota Singh heard that talk and adopted a unique technique to demoralize the government. They decided to prove that the announcement made by the government was wrong. They were lying and fooling the people. The two Sikhs occupied the road and declared that Khalsa were the rulers of Punjab. To spread this message to the people in the region, they started collecting a nominal toll from travelers using the road. They also sent an open message to the Governor, the Khan, just to make a joke of the government.

"Tell poor Khan that Baba Bota Singh is ruling the state with his heavy stick. He charges one nickel for a cart load and a penny for a donkey-load."

The people would pay this small amount without any grudge. They talked about the bravery of the Sikhs and the lies of the government when they went to their villages. After some days, the government sent well armed troops to catch the Sikhs. The Sikhs fought bravely, killing many soldiers, finally obtaining martyrdom themselves. They established the heroism of the Sikhs and proved that Sikhs were active and alive.

State terrorism can never kill the people's voice of truth.

8

SHAHEEDS

BHAI SUKHA SINGH

and

BHAI MEHTAB SINGH

Daring deeds Khalsa ploy
Evil they always destroy

Bhai Sukha Singh belonged to the village Mari Kamboki and Bhai Mehtab Singh belonged to the village Meeran Kote, both in the district of Amritsar. These two brave saint soldiers are famous for their daring deed of cutting the head of an evil man, Massa Rangar who was desecrating the Golden Temple in 1740.

Zakaria Khan, irritated by the Sikhs' resistance and his failure to subdue them, obtained the orders from Nadar Shah Durrani to annihilate the Sikhs from Punjab. Accordingly, it was advertised that if a person helps to catch or kill a Sikh, he would be rewarded handsomely. To steal and rob from Sikhs was made legal.

These orders of the government motivated many greedy people to become traitors. Cart-loads of severed heads of the Sikhs were sent to Lahore by such people to win government rewards. These traitors included Harbhagat Niranjania Chowdhary (a petty village official) of Majitha, Chowdhary of Noshaira Pannu, and Chowdhary

Massa Rangar of Mandiali. Of all these men, Massa was the most notorious and in charge of the Amritsar circle. He desecrated the Golden Temple by smoking and drinking inside there while watching dancing girls. Armed watchmen were posted around for his safety.

When the Sikhs in Bikaner heard about the desecration of their holy place of worship they became very angry. Bhai Sukha Singh and Bhai Mehtab Singh decided to go to Amritsar and stop the desecration. When they reached the gates of the city, they obtained baked-clay pots and broke them into small pieces. The broken clay pieces were rounded to look like coins of those days. The "coins" were put in small bags and the Sikhs dressed as village land revenue collectors, were ready to perform their task.

During those days, collectors would obtain revenue from the people of the villages in their charge and deposit the money with the local administrator who would send the collections to Lahore. The land revenue was paid in the form of coins of different values.

When the Sikhs reached the Golden Temple they passed by the watchmen without anyone even lifting a finger against them. The watchmen assumed by seeing the "coin bags" that the two village collectors were going to the Chowdhary for depositing their money. When the Sikhs got inside the Harimandar Sahib the bags were put before Massa, who was drunk and watching the dances of the girls. When he bent to feel the "coins" in the bags, a sword fell like lightning and cut off his head which was picked up by the Sikhs. Before the people inside or outside the Temple could compose themselves and know what had happened, the Sikhs on their horses had vanished. The job was performed so successfully that it brought great shame to the administration and the police of Amritsar.

The Nawab of Lahore got extremely angry and wanted to punish the Sikhs severely to take revenge of that insult. It was in 1745 when Mehtab Singh came to his village, that a traitor reported the matter secretly to the government. The police came quickly and surrounded the village before Bhai Mehtab Singh could go back to the forest. He was caught and brought to Lahore and was murdered by being crushed between rotating wheels with sharp teeth (charkhari).

Bhai Sukha Singh attained his martyrdom in 1753 while fighting the Mughal army on the banks of the river Ravi.

The daring deeds of Bhai Sukha Singh and Bhai Mehtab Singh tell us how brave and smart the Khalsa saint soldiers can be.

Khalsa are the daring, brave and smart saint soldiers of the Akal Purakh to fight against the oppression by the tyrants.

9

SHAHEED

BHAI TARU SINGH

Khalsa love and respect their hair.
They may be murdered, they do not care.

Sikhs had to leave their homes in the 18th century because of the constant attacks on them by the state police. Some Sikhs, however, remained in villages with the support of local Muslims. Bhai Taru Singh of Amritsar was one such Sikh. He was a farmer who used to help every needy person whether a Muslim, a Hindu or a Sikh. Poor people could depend upon him for support. He sent food and other necessities to the Khalsa living in the nearby forests.

Harbhagat Niranjania, filled with enmity for Sikhs and feeling jealous of Bhai Taru Singh made many false complaints to the government at Lahore. He hoped to get awards from the government for being their loyal informant. Finally, he succeeded in his evil mission. He brought police with him and had Bhai Taru Singh arrested and taken to Lahore in 1745. Zakaria Khan, the governor of Lahore, ordered the torture of Bhai Taru Singh. He remained calm and suffered all pain without changing his mind. After some time, when produced before Khan, Bhai Sahib asked the reasons for torturing him, particularly when he had committed no crime and was liked by all the people of his village.

Zakaria Khan told Bhai Taru Singh that a popular person like him should be a Muslim. Therefore, if he wanted to be free, he would have to adopt Islam. Further, Zakaria assured him that a good person like him would be very much honored by the government if he became a Muslim. However, Bhai Sahib stuck to his faith and refused to give it up at any cost. When the governor repeated his proposal with a firm order that Bhai Taru Singh had to choose either death or Islam, Bhai Sahib asked him, "You are assuring me you will spare my life if I become a Muslim but can you assure me that having become a Muslim I will live forever? Are you sure, being a Muslim you will never face death? If one has to die, sooner or later, then I would love to stick to my faith whatever you may like to do to me."

The Governor was angered at this reply of Bhai Taru Singh and therefore ordered the removal of his scalp. A barber was called for this purpose. The dreadful scene frightened everyone there including Zakaria Khan, himself. The watching of the horrible act of separating the scalp of a living man left a very terrifying picture in the mind of Zakaria Khan. He became sick and died soon after. Even many Muslims cursed him for his terrorism particularly against innocent people.

We must live and die as Sikhs as nothing is better than that. Tyrants who commit violence on innocent people to satisfy their evil mind, get themselves punished by their evil thoughts.

PART III

SHAHEED

SIKH WOMEN

The trainees at the Sikh Youth Camp observed that sakhis of brave Sikh women should also be included along with the sakhis of Sikh martyrs. Accordingly, these sakhis[*] have been included in Part III of this book.

[*]They are based mostly on the material given in "Sikh Women, Special Edition (Punjabi) of Singh Sabha Pattarka" published by Kendri Sri Guru Singh Sabha, Amritsar.

1

MAI BHAG KAUR

Mai Bhag Kaur, popularly known as Mai Bhago, was born in village Jhabal, near Amritsar. She was the grand-daughter of Bhai Paro Shah, brother of Bhai Langaha, who served Guru Arjan Dev and Guru Har Gobind Ji.

As a young girl, she heard the *sakhis* of the martyrdom of Guru Arjan Dev and of army attacks on Guru Har Gobind. State terrorism against the Gurus and the Sikhs was often talked about in the family. Her two generations were closely involved with it because they had personally experienced it while serving the Gurus. A regular hearing of the *sakhis* of injustices done to the Sikhs and their harassment by the police and army made a deep effect on her tender heart.

Mai Bhago was still a child when she heard *sakhis* of Guru Tegh Bahadur and three Sikhs, Bhai Dayala, Bhai Mati Das and Bhai Sati Das who were tortured and murdered at Delhi in 1675. The sad news touched her heart and she decided in her mind to do her duty to stop such state violence against the Sikhs. This thought grew stronger and stronger in her mind as she grew into her teens.

She went to Anandpur Sahib along with her father in 1699 when Guru Gobind Singh founded the Khalsa Panth. She took Amrit and wanted to stay there to learn the art of fighting and self defense. But, her father brought her to their village because she was a woman and not a man to go to the fighting lines. In her mind, however, she continued to nurse the idea of joining the Khalsa forces.

After returning to her village, she started learning martial art, particularly the use of the spear. She would go to a nearby forest reserve and practice piercing trees with her spear. She soon became an expert in the art of using this handy weapon in battle.

Government forces surrounded Anandpur in 1704 but they could not defeat the Guru or make him to vacate the city. Finally to save their face with the emperor, they under a written oath, requested the Guru to leave Anandpur without being harmed by them. They agreed not only to let the Guru move out of Anandpur to anywhere he liked to go, but also to let him come and stay at Anandpur again after some time. They wrote to the Guru that their only aim was to make the Guru to leave Anandpur at that time and that they had no intention of harming the Guru.

The generals, however, broke their oath and attacked the Guru when he came out of the fort. He was forced to fight the battles while crossing the river Sirsa and at a nearby village Chamkaur where many of his Sikhs and his two elder sons became martyrs. They, however, could not harm the person of the Guru.

The news that the Guru had left Anandpur and was coming to Malwa made Mai Bhago to do what she was thinking since long. She went from village to village to inform the Sikhs and organize them to challenge the army following the Guru. While addressing people in a village she would tell them, "Our Guru has sacrificed all his family for our freedom. Why can't we ourselves stand up and protect our own civil and human rights?" Her sharp words awakened the souls of many men. They would wonder at the bravery of a woman going around courageously and making people to get together for claiming their rights and fighting for justice.

Mai Bhag Kaur and hundreds of men with her were planning their strategy when the news came that the Guru was proceeding towards a lake, Khidrana Di Dhab, now called Mukatsar and the Mughal Army was following him. They decided to check the army from reaching the lake, the only source of water for many miles around. The Guru with some Sikhs occupied the top of the mound on the bank of the lake. Mai Bhag Kaur and the Sikhs with her organized themselves around the lake.

When the army arrived at the lake and attacked the Sikhs, they were ready to beat them back. A bloody battle took place. Mai showed her bravery by fighting with the soldiers in the front lines. She would use her spear with a smart move. Before a soldier could get ready to attack her, he was down on earth with his chest pierced by her spear. The mercenary soldiers could not face the devoted Sikhs. The Guru from the mound provided the necessary support with his snake like arrows. The army generals soon found that unless they retreated quickly all of them would find their grave yard in the battle field and none would return alive. Historians say that they left even their wounded soldiers unattended and returned as fast as they could. This was the last battle the Mughal army could dare to fight with the Guru.

After the battle was won, the Guru came down from the mound and took care of the wounded and the dead. Mai Bhag Kaur was lying badly injured. She was treated carefully and she soon became healthy. When the Guru asked her to go back to her village along with other Sikhs, she told the Guru her long cherished desire to become an active Saint-soldier in the army of the Guru. Her wishes were granted and the Guru agreed to let her stay with him as a member of his body-guard.

Along with the Guru, she went to Nanded in the south of India and lived there for the rest of her life. There is a Gurdwara where she lived at Nanded, near the Gurdwara Sachkand, built in memory of the Guru. It reminds the visitors of her devotion and services to the Guru.

Like Sikh men, Sikh women are equally good saint-soldiers. They can organize men and lead them to fight and win battles for the freedom of people and their human rights.

2

WOMEN MARTYRS

OF SHAHEED GANJ, LAHORE

Guru Nanak Dev, the founder of Sikhism, preached equality of humanity. He taught his disciples to "see" God in every human being. To put his philosophy into practice, he started the institutions of *sangat* and *pangat* where all people would sit together, pray together, and eat together without any kind of discrimination. All people, Hindus, Muslims, and so-called low castes loved the Guru as their own. To express the love of the people for Guru Nanak, a folk rhyme, *Nanak Shah Fakir, Hindu Ka Guru, Musalman Ka Pir*, became popular with the masses. By the time of Guru Amar Das , Sikhism became a mass movement.

The government started worrying lest the people get themselves organized under the guidance of the Guru and revolt against their rule of injustice. It was under this fear, that Guru Arjan Dev was arrested, tortured and murdered in 1606. From then on, state terrorism continued against the Sikhs even beyond the middle of the 18th century. The strength of the Khalsa and the faith of the people in the righteousness of the Sikhs, however, went on increasing as the terrorism against them was intensified by the government. Finally, the people did throw away the cruel rule and welcomed the Khalsa government lead by Maharaja Ranjit Singh over north-west India. The Sikhs, though, did not make even 10% of the population at that time.

This *sakhi* belongs to the period of Mir Mannu, Governor of Lahore (1748 -1753). During that period the looting, torturing and killing of Sikhs was made legal and the killers were rewarded by the government . The Punjab was attacked for the third time by Ahmed Shah Abdali, the ruler of Afghanistan, in December 1751. Mannu was defeated and the province of Punjab was taken over by the Afghans from the Delhi Emperor. Kaura Mal, a Minister of Mannu, but a friend of the Sikhs was killed in the battle. Thus, the only link between misldars (Sikh chiefs) and Mannu was lost. No body was left to hold Mannu from executing his evil ideas and ill motives against the Sikhs.

When Mannu was busy with Abdali, Sikhs consolidated their hold on the areas under their control. This irritated Mannu very much. Further, the frustration of his defeat at the hands of Abdali, was converted into anger against the Sikhs. He sent army bands to hunt the Sikhs, catch them or kill them.

In March 1753, the commander of Jallandhar lead his army on the Sikhs and killed a great many of them gathering for Hola Mahalla at Anandpur. Mannu attacked Ram Rauni, a fort of Sikhs at Amritsar. He blew up the fort and killed all the 900 Sikhs there. Army bands were sent out to search and kill Sikhs. Skirmishes between the roving bands and the Sikh *jatha*s were a common occurrence.

The sympathy of the people was with the Sikhs but the control of the army was in the hands of Mannu. It was not difficult for the Sikhs to dodge the army men and move to inaccessible places in the jungles or into sedges along the river beds. Not finding the Sikhs in their houses and not being able to follow them to their hiding places, the army men would pick up their women and children. They were brought to Lahore, tortured and murdered in cold blood in Nakhas market for horses.

Miskin, personal attendant of Mannu, has given an eye witness account of the violence against the Sikhs, in the following words:

Mannu appointed most of his soldiers to the task of chastising the Sikhs. They ran after these wretches up to 28 Kos (approximately a Kos is one and a half mile) in a day and slew them wherever they stood up to oppose them. Everyone who brought Sikh heads to Mannu received a reward of Rupees 10 per head. Anyone who brought a horse belonging to a Sikh could keep it as his own. Whosoever lost his own horse by chance in the fight with the Sikhs got another in its place from the government stable.

The persons who brought Sikhs alive or their heads or their horses received prizes. The Sikhs who were captured alive were sent to hell by being beaten with wooden mallets. At times Adina Beg Khan sent 40 or 50 Sikh captives from Doab Jallandhar. they were as a rule killed with the strokes of wooden hammers.

Sometime Mannu himself rode a horse and went hunting for Sikhs. Once, when his men fired a volley on Sikhs hiding in a sugarcane field, his horse got scared. It suddenly jumped up and ran away. Mannu fell from his horse, but his foot got caught in the saddle. Dragged by his horse, Mannu lost his life.

Inhuman tortures were given to the Sikh women and children brought to Lahore to force them to change their faith. Not a single person submitted to the cruel government. All of them, without a sorrow, suffered all kinds of pain and death.

The women were kept hungry and forced to grind grain by working heavy stone mills. The minimum ration was given to them so that they did not die of hunger, but were able to keep on living and suffering tortures. To break their will and high spirits, they were made to watch their children being thrown up in the air to fall back on the sharp blades of spears. Children pierced through by the spears were cut into pieces and put as a necklace around the necks of their mothers. The dogs were permitted to eat their flesh before the eyes of their helpless mothers. These great women bore all this without even a sigh on their lips.

The martyrdom and unparalleled sacrifices of the great Sikh women and their children are remembered by Sikhs in their prayer *"Let us remember the women who suffered in the jail of Mannu, remained hungry, worked heavy stone mills, watched their children being pierced by the spears and got their body pieces around their necks ... keeping their sacrifices in mind let all of us hail them and say Waheguru."*

In memory of those martyrs, there now stands Gurdwara Shaheed Ganj, Lahore.

Sikhs, while undergoing all these cruelties kept their morale and spirits high. To express there feelings, there is a folk saying of that period:

We are like plants and Mannu a sickle, all know.
The more he cuts us, the more we grow.

As an outcome of these sacrifices for human rights, people developed a great regard for the Sikhs and nursed sincere sympathy for them. Finally, the tyrannical rule ended and with the support of the masses, the Sikhs became the rulers of the state.

3

SARDARNI SADA KAUR

Sardarni Sada Kaur, mother-in-law of Maharaja Ranjit Singh, is one of the builders of the Sikh Raj. She was born to Sardar Dasaunda Singh of Ferozepur District and was married to Sardar Gurbakhsh Singh son of Sardar Jai Singh, jathedar (Head) of the Ghanya Misl. The misls, were a kind of kingdom of the Sikh sardars. They collected revenue from their Misl areas.

Sardar Jai Singh was a friend of Sardar Charhat Singh, the Jathedar of the Shakarchakia Misl. The areas of the two Misls were adjacent to each other. Unfortunately, Sardar Charhat Singh died early leaving his young son, Mahan Singh, an orphan. Sardar Jai Singh extended his sympathy to the bereaved family and raised Mahan Singh with love and affection.

When Mahan Singh became an adult, he wanted to use his powers to increase his revenues. He collected money from the nearby Jammu area, which was under the protection of Sardar Jai Singh. Naturally, he got angry at the young boy, Mahan Singh, for his unfaithful act. He ordered him to pay a heavy fine or be ready to be attacked and turned out of his Misl area.

Mahan Singh understood the blunder he made for the lust of wealth. He went to Jai Singh to feel sorry and negotiate the fine to be paid by him. Sardar Jai Singh, being very mad, did not agree to relax his condition of collecting heavy fines from Mahan Singh. The reconciliation efforts having failed, he had no alternative but to face the mighty Sardar Jai Singh. To be able to come up to the level of giving a good fight to Jai Singh, the young sardar decided to get as many people on his side as possible. All the opponents and Sikh chiefs jealous of Jai Singh got on the side of Mahan Singh.

A big battle was fought between the two brave Sikh armies, each proud of his men and their expertise in fighting skills. Gurbakhsh Singh, son of Jai Singh was fighting on one front independent of his father. He was murdered in the fight, leaving young Sardarni Sada Kaur a widow and his father without support. Jai Singh could not bear the loss of his only son in the battle and immediately gave up the fight. He threw away his arms and raising his hands cried aloud to his opponent to murder him. While weeping he said he did not want to live without his son, his only hope in the world. The fighting stopped right away leaving Jai Singh a mental wreck and incapable of managing his Misl.

Sardarni Sada Kaur did not lose her heart even under these trying and adverse situations. She decided to face all these problems bravely and tactfully. She reconciled with her main opponent Mahan Singh. She offered the hand of her daughter Mehtab Kaur to Ranjit Singh, the son of Mahan Singh. The engagement of the two children cemented the friendship of their parents and removed all the grains of mutual enmity and misgivings. The combination of the two big Misls, Shakarchakia and Ghanya created a force to be counted as number one in the Punjab state.

It is said misfortunes never come alone. Another great tragedy struck Sada Kaur. Sardar Mahan Singh died three years after the engagement of his son Ranjit Singh and left him an orphan at the age of nine. To face this new unfortunate situation, Sardarni Sada Kaur had to perform the marriage ceremony for her daughter when she was just a child. The marriage entitled her to conduct and manage the affairs of the Shakarchakia Misl as well.

She handled her job so wisely and bravely that she was able to achieve the long cherished goal of the Sikhs of becoming the rulers of Punjab. She performed this great task within 9 years after taking over the charge of the two Misls.

She used both tact and power to unite all the major Misls to take over the rule of Punjab. Some Sikh chiefs willingly joined her because of her good negotiating power. Others, she physically took over with the help of her strong army and annexed their Misls. She gave them (Sikh chiefs defeated by her) appropriate positions in the enlarged kingdom to keep them on her side rather than letting them nurse any ill-will against her as her opponents.

Whenever an opponent tried to weaken her or any invader tried to loot her territory, she defeated them to silence them for ever. In this way one success after the other, led her to make her son-in-law, Ranjit Singh, to be the ruler of Lahore before the turn of the century. The Sikh Raj was thus established in 1799 in Punjab. She guided, advised, and helped him to take over not only the whole of Punjab lying to the west of the Satlej River , but also to become the ruler of the regions adjacent to the Punjab. Ranjit Singh thus became a great powerful Maharaja of Punjab. He defeated the Pathans and Mughals, and subdued these great fighters who had been coming from the west, invading and looting Punjab for almost a century.

Sardarni Sada Kaur thus carved out a place for herself in the history of the North Western India as one of the builders of the Sikh State.

Sikh women are good statesmen and great soldiers. They can organize armies, win battles, and rule the state well.

4

SARDARNI

SHARNAGAT KAUR

The *sakhi* of this great Sikh woman starts from the very day of her marriage. She was born in a Hindu family in the Pathan country on the west of the Punjab. The area was under the Sikh Raj and ruled by General Hari Singh Nalwa.

After a happy marriage, she was going along with her groom and the marriage party to the village of her in-laws. On their way, the dacoits ambushed them. Waving their arms, the dacoits ordered all the people to surrender their cash and valuables. The helpless party gave everything to the robbers to save their lives. The dacoits, however, also demanded the newly married bride and took her with them.

The poor groom went straight to General Nalwa, the governor of the Pathan province. While the general sitting in his court was listening to the complaint of the groom, he observed two persons behaving suspiciously near the door. He suspected them to be the friends of the dacoits. After the man had completed the story of the marriage party being way-laid by the dacoits and the loss of his wife, the general ordered aloud to be heard by those suspects, "Put this man in prison. He did not care to protect a helpless woman, who was his own wife."

The two suspects were actually the associates of the dacoits and had come there to know the reactions of the general. Both were pleased to hear the orders. Having been relieved of the fear of any policemen going out in search of the dacoits to catch them, they could not conceal their happiness. The vigilant eyes of the general observed the smiles on the faces of the suspects when they heard his decision. This assured the general of their complicity in looting the marriage party and carrying away the bride. The general secretly ordered ten Sikh horsemen to take the husband of the abducted woman with them and follow the suspects.

Having been satisfied that the general was angry with the cowardly behavior of the groom, the associates of the dacoits assumed that the whole episode was over and forgotten. Therefore, they decided to go to the dacoits immediately and tell them the good news of the decision of the general. When they reached the house where the dacoits held the bride, they told them about the reactions of the general. They were talking joyfully when the horsemen surrounded the dacoits and ordered them to put their hands up. The dacoits wondered about the smart move of the general.

When the bride was brought before Sardar Nalwa he asked her, "What is your name?" She replied, "I am nobody. I would have been dead had you not saved my life. Now I am under your 'sharan' (protection). The word 'sharan' voluntarily coming out of the mouth of a helpless, scared woman gave her the popular name Sharanagat Kaur.

When everything including the robbed ornaments was restored to them, the general asked the bride and groom to go home. Both begged the Sardar to admit them to the Khalsa Panth. They wanted to enjoy the honor of living as Sikhs and dying as Sikhs. On their very firm resolve to become the members of the Khalsa Panth, they were given Amrit and allowed to stay there.

Once Hari Singh Nalwa was visiting Jamrod Fort. He fell seriously ill there. The area was surrounded with the Pathan population unfriendly towards him. Knowing that the general was sick and not physically in a condition to engage himself in battle, they all rebelled against his rule. To send the message that he was hale and hearty, the general went up to the upper story of the fort from where he could be seen by all the people outside the fort. Seeing him moving about on the fort, the rebels retreated quickly. However, one of them aimed his gun at him and shot him. Unfortunately, the general was hit and died of the bullet wound.

The situation in the fort became very tense and everyone was depressed finding their general dead, and with no one there to replace him. Bibi Sharanagat Kaur kept her composure, thought for some time and said, "This is not the time to feel worried or to get scared. Let us face this critical moment with courage and confidence. I have a plan to save the situation. You drop me behind the fort by a long rope. I, disguised as a Pathan woman, will reach Peshawar as soon as possible and inform the army there''.

She had to travel through a hilly route that covered twenty miles, swarming with Pathan rebels. There were wild animals in the forest through which she had to walk at night, and she could easily become their prey. It was a very risky journey. It looked impossible for a woman to reach Peshawar alive under those conditions and give the sad news to the army and to request their help.

The brave, daring young woman did reach there by walking and running the whole night, through dense forest. Without losing any time, she asked the best horsemen to get ready quickly and ride their horses. Sikh soldiers under the guidance of Bibi Sharanagat Kaur traveled as fast as they could to reach Lahore. They covered their long arduous journey quickly and reported the episode to Maharaja Ranjeet Singh.

After hearing of the death of a great general who raised the honor of the Khalsa army to the skies, he felt very sad. Assessing the situation to be critical, he himself left for Peshawar. Knowing that the Maharaja had personally come to punish the rebels, the Pathans immediately surrendered without fighting and promised to remain friendly thereafter.

The Khalsa Raj of Punjab, founded with the statesmanship of a woman, Sardarni Sada Kaur, was thus saved from being dismembered, by the bravery of another woman, Bibi Sharanagat Kaur. She was honored by the Khalsa Panth with the title of "Brave daughter of the Punjab."

Sikh women can successfully face all kinds of critical and risky situations, like any good general and statesman.

5

MATA

KISHAN KAUR KAONKE

This is the *sakhi* of a brave woman who lived in this century and whose life was devoted to the Sikh Panth. She was born in 1856 and was the daughter of Sardar Suba Singh of Village Lohgarh in Ludhiana district. While living in her village, she learned Gurbani and Sikh history from the *granthi ji* of the Gurdwara there. She was married to Sardar Harnam Singh of Village Kaonke. He later on joined the army and died in 1902 while serving in Burma. Her two sons had also died when they were still young. She was thus left a widow and without any offspring. Rather than bearing the curses of Hindu society of being a widow or feeling lonely, she decided to spend the rest of her life in the service of the Khalsa Panth.

In 1903, Mata Kishan Kaur went to Gurdwara Sach Khand, Nanded in the south of India. The Gurdwara was built in the memory of Guru Gobind Singh who left for his heavenly abode from there. She stayed at Nanded for some time, took Amrit to become a saint-soldier of the Khalsa Panth and started tying a turban on her head. She devoted herself to organizing people to preach and practised the equality of men and women and the so-called low castes and high castes of the Hindu society.

After the death of her husband, his brother did not let her take over the possession of her share of land. When other methods failed, she went to the fields and personally told the brother of her husband to leave the fields for her. Finding her alone and helpless in the fields, he made some vulgar jokes, and did not leave the fields. She was courageous and a brave person. She raised her strong arm and fixed a hard slap on his face. The man, feeling guilty of his misbehavior and being hit hard by an upright woman ran away to avoid a second slap from her. Mata Kaonke took over the possession of the land which belonged to her. She was respected by the whole village as a great lady of good behavior, with great courage.

When the Khalsa Panth started the Gurdwara Freedom Movement in the beginning of this century, she joined the movement as an active worker. In 1920, the Mahants refused offerings of some Sikhs who were recent converts from the so-called low-castes. She was with the Sikhs who went to the Golden Temple to protest against this anti-Sikh behavior of the Mahants. She was there to physically set the Mahants straight if they did not listen to their arguments. Observing the mood of the Sikhs, the Mahants fled from the Gurdwara leaving it vacant for the Sikhs to occupy and take over its control.

In September 1922, during Guru Ka Bagh Morcha, Sikhs were beaten by police and even run over by the mounted police, breaking the bones of Sikhs under the hooves of their horses. Mata Ji and her associates undertook the sewa of caring for the injured Sikhs, taking them to the hospitals, and nursing them there. Every day she would go with the *jatha* to the Guru Ka Bagh. The policemen would beat the Sikhs with lathis to stop them from going to the Bagh. The police would let the attending Sikhs carry the injured members of the protesting *jatha*. It is then that Mai Kishan Kaur took over the duty of administering first aid to them and taking them to the hospital.

One day, a very large number of Sikhs suffered very severe injuries. The police chief taunted her by telling her that there was much sewa for her to do. Mata Ji was already feeling very much hurt to see the Sikhs being tortured and beaten like that. After hearing the taunting words of the police chief, she could no longer restrain herself. In response to his comments, she took a few firm daring steps towards the police chief, and looking at him with ferocious eyes, she raised her arm and like a lightning bolt, hit him in the face.

The strong unexpected slap shook the police chief and turned his face over his shoulder. Without giving the brave woman a second look, he ran towards his tent to save his face from the second slap. This was a great insult not only for all of the police force, but for the whole British government.

Hearing of the tortures committed on the innocent Sikhs and the bearing of atrocities by them, gave Father C.F. Andrews, a Christian missionary, the courage to come to Guru Ka Bagh. After seeing the anti-human behavior of the British police officers, he cried, "I see hundreds of Christs being crucified every day by the Christians themselves." This changed the direction of the Morcha and finally the government yielded to permit the Sikhs their legal rights by owning the Guru Ka Bagh lands.

Mata Kaonke again performed a daring deed during Jaito Morcha. Sikhs wanted to continue the Akhand Path disrupted by the police by arresting all the Sikhs there. A *jatha* of 500 Sikhs marched from the Akal Takhat in Amritsar to Gurdwara Jaito. People knew the *jatha* would be handled brutally by the police. To know the truth and details of the brutalities Mata Kaonke dressed herself as a Jain woman and moved into the police camp. The government forces rained bullets on the *jatha*. The police secretly disposed of the dead bodies and removed the injured to the hospitals. They issued totally misleading reports and did not give the correct information about the Sikhs killed and injured. Mata Kaonke had seen all the actions with her own eyes and she made the facts public. When the details revealed by her were found to be true, the government was very much embarrassed, and was also very much surprised. After some time the secret police traced her and charged her with espionage. She was sentenced to four years in jail.

In 1925, the government accepted their defeat in the struggle against the Sikhs. They agreed to the formation of a Sikh body which would take over the management of the Gurdwaras from the Mahants who were under the control of the government. With this agreement, all the persons arrested in connection with the Gurdwara movement were released. Mata Kaonke, however, had to remain in jail until 1928 to undergo her full sentence.

When released from jail, she went straight to the Akal Takhat to express her thanks to the Guru for giving her a chance to serve the Khalsa Panth. She suffered for the cause of the Sikhs and freedom of the Gurdwaras from the government control. The Khalsa Panth honored her at the Akal Takhat and gave her the title of Mata. Since then she became popular as Mata Kishan Kaur.

During the rest of her life, she stayed at her village, built a Gurdwara there and preached the Sikh faith to the people in the region. She died at the age of 96 in 1952.

The life spent in the service of society is fruitful. Sikh women can accomplish this by overcoming their personal and family limitations.

Bhai Mati Das

Bhai Subeg Singh, Bhai Shehbaz Singh

Bhai Taru Singh Ji (July 1, 1745)

Zakari Khan and Mir Mannu

A moving picture of the Sikh mothers who were forced to wear the mangled limbs of their slaughtered children, yet never let their faith be undetermined.

Bhai Mani Singh (1662-1739)

Baba Deep Singh Ji (1682-1757)

Baba Bota Singh and Garja Singh

Baba Banda Singh Bahadur (1670-1716)

PART IV

SEWA

Do Sewa, Sewa Leads to Success.
Sewa means listen to the Guru and obey him.

1

To your Guru ever say yes.
Obedience to him leads to success.

(i)

BHAI LEHNA

Guru Nanak Dev founded a new village and named it Kartarpur. The Guru used to do farming there. He held his daily meetings with the people in the village to tell them about God and the goal of human life. Bhai Lehna, a resident of village Khadur, believed in the worship of the goddess, Vaishnav Devi. Once during his annual trip to that goddess, he wanted to meet the Guru, as well. Bhai Lehna reached Kartarpur, heard his preaching and finally received the peace for which he had so long been searching. He, therefore, gave up his regular pilgrimage to the goddess, and decided to settle at Kartarpur to enjoy and follow the preaching of the Guru, and thus, realize the goal of his life.

During his stay at Kartarpur, Bhai Lehna remained in the service of the Guru. He did everything the Guru wished him to do. In this way he became one of the very close followers of the Guru.

There are many *sakhis* about the obedience of Bhai Lehna telling us how he gave up his ego and followed the path shown by the Guru. He was never reluctant to do what the Guru wanted the Sikhs, the disciples, to do. Two *sakhis* given below, tell us about the sincere love and commitment of Bhai Lehna for the Guru.

1) One day while working in the rice fields, some grass growing in the crop was removed. It was to be fed to the animals in the house. The Guru asked his sons, Bhai Sri Chand and Bhai Lakhmi Chand to carry the bundle home. They declined to do that because the muddy water dripping from the wet roots of the grass would spoil their clothes. When the Guru looked towards Bhai Lehna, he immediately picked up the bundle of grass and brought it home. This act of devotion by Bhai Lehna pleased the Guru very much.

2) Once Guru Nanak Dev was taking a bath and while doing so, the cup he used for pouring water on his body slipped and rolled into a pit containing dirty water. When asked to take out the cup, the sons of the Guru advised him to get that dirty job done by someone else. Bhai Lehna, however, did not mind at all. He put his hand in the dirty water, took out the cup, cleaned it and handed it over to the Guru.

The thorough destruction of his ego and his complete obedience to the Guru made Bhai Lehna suitable to be chosen as the second Nanak. Before his death, Guru Nanak Dev passed on the responsibility of the guruship to Bhai Lehna and named him Angad Dev.

Obedience to the Guru is the first step on the path to God.

(ii)

BABA AMAR DAS

Guru Nanak Dev, the founder of the Sikh faith, chose Bhai Lehna as his successor to preach love of God and brotherhood of humanity. At the ceremony of installing Bhai Lehna as the second Guru, he was given a new name, Angad Dev. Having appointed Guru Angad Dev as his successor, Guru Nanak asked him to move to his own village, Khadoor. At this new Sikh center, he was to popularize the institutions of *sangat* and *pangat*, the two major pillars of the faith, established by Guru Nanak.

Accordingly, Guru Angad Dev started the second Sikh Center at his village situated on the western bank of the river Beas. Baba Amar Das, about 25 years older than the Guru, came to him to learn the teachings of the Sikh faith. Baba Ji was the brother of the father-in-law of Bibi Amro, the daughter of the Guru.

Baba Amar Das was told to recite Gurbani, listen to kirtan and to do *sewa* (volunteer service). He was assigned the responsibility of *langar*, a free kitchen open to all people. It was a hard job to do at the age of 60 years. Baba Ji would get up early in the morning, go down to the river about a kilometer away, fill the pitcher with water, and walk up to the village with the heavy load on his head. He recited Gurbani during his daily trip to the river.

His second job was to get himself busy with the preparation of the morning *langar*, cooking pulses and vegetables for the *sangat*. When all the members of the *sangat* had been served food, it was his turn to eat. As soon as the *langar* service was over, the cleaning

78

of utensils and sweeping of the floor drew his attention.

When he was through with the *langar* sewa, it was time for him to go to the forest. Baba Ji would pick up an ax and move out. In the jungle, he collected dry fuel wood, chopped it into small pieces and tied them into a bundle. With the load of wood on his head, he was ready for his journey back to the village .

Returning to the *langar* building, Baba Ji would kindle fire and start cooking evening meals. He performed all the necessary chores for preparing food for *sangat* by the time the evening prayers were over. All the visitors would sit in *pangat* (row) for being served *langar*. It gave a lot of happiness to Baba Amar Das to feed people visiting the Guru. When everyone had left, and the utensils were cleaned and put back in their places, it was time for him to rest for the night. Though *langar sewa* was a difficult job, it was a source of satisfaction for Baba Ji. He attended to this hard job with devotion and commitment for more than a decade.

A new assignment was waiting for this great disciple of the Guru. It was the establishment of another Sikh center about four miles down the stream, where there was a ford. The highway which connected Delhi, the capital of India, and Lahore, the capital of Punjab, passed through this place. Travelers crossed the river at this spot. On the right bank of the river was a piece of land which belonged to Gonda, a disciple of the Guru. He offered it to Guru Angad Dev for establishing a center there. The Guru deputed Baba Amar Das Ji to dig a *baoli*, an open well with steps leading to the water level, to provide water for all the residents.

Baba Ji had been strictly obeying the Guru and serving *sangat* with zeal for more than 12 years when he was nominated as the third Nanak. Guru Angad Dev invited Baba Budha Ji, a Sikh blessed by Guru Nanak Dev, to perform the ceremony. Baba Amar Das was seated on a prominent place visible to all the *sangat*. Guru

Angad Dev bowed before him declaring him to be the third Nanak. The mark of honor on his forehead was made by Bhai Budha Ji.

Having been nominated Guru, Baba Ji continued to develop the third Sikh center and made it his headquarters. To honor Bhai Gonda, who offered that land to the Guru, the place was named Goindwal.

(iii)

BHAI JETHA JI

Guru Amar Das undertook a big job of establishing a new Sikh center, Goindwal. It was named after the owner, Gonda, who offered the land for this purpose. The Guru belonged to the village named Basarkay. There lived a young orphan boy popular as Bhai Jetha. The Guru loved him a lot and asked him to move to Goindwal.

Bhai Jetha was born at Chuna Mandi, Lahore. Being the first child born to his parents, he was named Jetha, which means the first or the oldest. The boy was still a child when both his parents died. Therefore, his maternal grandmother brought him to her village Basarkay. Baba Amar Das lived nearby in the same village. He developed great sympathy and affection for this sweet and obedient child. Baba Ji was very much interested in the welfare of Bhai Jetha. When the construction work started at Goindwal, the boy and her grandmother were suggested to move to the new place.

Bhai Jetha took up the profession of boiling chickpeas, and selling them to the people in the village. This way, he made a meager earning for himself and his grandmother who looked after him. During the rest of the time, Bhai Jetha did the *sewa* of digging earth for building the Baoli. His innocence, intelligence and sweet temperament were liked by everyone. Keeping in mind the good nature of the boy and his love for doing *sewa*, Guru Amar Das married his daughter, Bibi Bhani to this young disciple.

His new status, the son-in-law of the Guru, made him more

humble and more responsible. After his marriage, Bhai Jetha continued to do *sewa* regularly for as much time as he could. He was also deputed by the Guru to copy Gurbani hymns written by the previous Gurus. In one of the copies (called Goindwal Pothian) we find his signatures as Ghulam Jetha Chand. Ghulam means a slave. This tells us about the commitment he had for serving the Guru. His exemplary obedience to the Guru was famous among all disciples living in the village or working there. The elder daughter of the Guru was married to Bhai Rama, who too was a noble soul. He was respected by the Sikhs for his good behavior.

Everyday more and more people adopted the new faith founded by Guru Nanak. The Sikh community had grown quite large by the time of Guru Amar Das. To meet the religious needs of the followers of this fast growing faith, 22 sub-centers were established by the Guru. A sub-center was called a *manji*. This name became popular because the person in charge of the region used to sit on a *manji*, a cot, to preach to the disciples.

Now, the Guru decided to found the main Sikh center for the ever increasing Sikh community. A suitable piece of land was chosen in the middle of Majha, the tract lying between the rivers of Beas and Ravi. It was a low lying place in that region. The Guru deputed Bhai Jetha to dig there a huge *sarovar*, a sacred pool.

One day when the Guru was about to leave this world, he called both Bhai Rama and Bhai Jetha. He told each of them to build a platform for him to sit on while preaching to the *sangat*. Both devoted themselves to the sewa and the platforms were ready in a few days. The Guru examined both the structures but did not approve of them. He desired that the platforms be demolished and re-built. Accordingly, the platforms were built again with greater care. However, the Guru repeated his previous orders and wanted the platforms to be re-constructed.

The tradition says Bhai Rama gave it up saying that that was the best he could do. However Bhai Jetha Ji requested the Guru to excuse him for his incompetence. He felt sorry that he could not come up to the expectations of the Guru and he started to re-build the structure. Obviously this humility, devotion to *sewa* and extreme type of obedience to the Guru raised him to the highest status, the Guruship. Guru Amar Das sent for Baba Budha Ji, the same holy person, who performed the Guruship ceremony in his own case. On the arrival of Bhai Budha Ji, all the *sangat* gathered to watch an orphan boy, who had become an embodiment of *sewa*, being rewarded as Guru. Guru Amar Das, though father-in-law of Bhai Jetha Ji, bowed before him and declared him to be his successor. Baba Budha Ji put a mark on his forehead and he was re-named Guru Ram Das.

After the ceremony, Guru Ram Das moved to the spot chosen for constructing the pool and continued his *sewa*. The place was first called Chak Ram Das and later Ram Das Pur. Now it is known as Amritsar and is famous all over the world for its *sarovar* and the Golden Temple. It is now the headquarters of the Sikh nation.

2

Nurse no ill will for others,
It hurts everyone and bothers.

(i)

YOGI

Guru Nanak Dev told his successor, Guru Angad Dev, to leave Kartarpur and move to his own village, Khadoor, to start another preaching center there.

Knowing about his return to the village, residents of Khadoor and nearby villages came to pay their respect to the Guru. They were all happy to have him among themselves, once again. Many people started coming there regularly, both in the morning and in the evening. They listened with devotion to the recitation of Gurbani and Kirtan (singing of hymns) performed there daily.

The Guru founded a school for teaching Gurmukhi script to the people. A center for physical activities was also started and wrestling bouts were held there. This made the Guru popular in the villages around there and he became the center of all activities in the region. People came to him to know the mission of human life and learn Sikh practices. All people were welcome to the congregation, without any kind of discrimination irrespective of their faith, caste or status.

A yogi, who lived outside the village and who used to get the attention of the villagers, felt jealous of the Guru. He found that the villagers were no longer interested in him. He adopted many techniques to attract some persons but all in vain. He decided to go on a long pilgrimage, a tour to religious places, and get blessings of the holy men living there. When he returned to Khadoor, he told stories about the people and the places he had visited. However, the villagers did not listen to him or show any desire to know about the holy places he had visited. This made the yogi very unhappy and more jealous of the Guru.

Incidentally, that year there was no rain. Crops started withering and people suffered a great shortage of drinking water. Yogi took advantage of this situation and blamed the Guru for it. He told people that God would not send rain to their village because they were committing a great sin by worshipping a family man as Guru. He argued, ''The Guru is married and has children. He cannot find time to meditate on God while remaining busy with his family responsibilities.''

Many such mischievous comments about the Guru were made by the yogi to give a set back to Guru's popularity. Further, he misguided the people by telling them that God would send rain only if the Guru was turned out of the village. The simple village folks were taken in by yogi's talks. They requested the Guru to bring rain. The Guru told them that the rain was in the hands of God, who alone decides His plan. The people mentioned to him the yogi's promise to bring rain if the Guru left the village. The Guru thought it desirable to expose the fake yogi. Accordingly, he left Khadoor that very moment and moved to another village.

When the Guru vacated the village, people went to the yogi and asked him to bring rain. The yogi was happy to have the Guru leave the village. He thought the people would have none else but him for presenting their offerings. For some days, he fed villagers on false promises that he would pray all night to bring rain. But the rain did not come and the people started losing their patience. After some days, they were not willing to wait any more. Whenever the people went to the yogi, he advised them to wait one more day, hoping the delayed rains would come any day.

Finally, the villagers were frustrated and disappointed. They challenged the yogi to either bring rain right at that time or be ready to be punched for cheating them. It was not in the hands of the yogi to bring rain. It is a gift of God. The pulling, punching and dragging of the yogi by the villagers resulted in the death of the jealous yogi.

It so happened that after the yogi was dead, clouds started covering the sky. Soon the clouds became thick and dark all over. Finally, it started raining.

The people believed that God did not send rain to give them the message that *He does not like jealous people*.

(ii)

TAPA

Guru Amar Das founded a new Sikh center at Goindwal. He dug a Baoli, an open well with steps reaching down to the water level. Everyone, a Hindu, a Muslim, a so-called low caste, poor or rich, was welcome to take water from that Baoli. This made all people live like one big brotherhood. The institutions of *sangat* and *pangat* had already become popular with the people. *Sangat* is a congregation of holy people sitting together as equals and singing praises of the lord; *pangat* means sitting together as equals and eating free food contributed voluntarily by the community. In addition to the popularization of these two institutions, Baoli was another step taken by the Guru to convey the message of the Sikh faith: *All people are equal. No one is high or low because of one's caste or wealth.*

People came to the Guru even from far off villages to listen to his teachings and enjoy the recitation of Gurbani. Everyone could join the congregation without any kind of discrimination. All would sit together in a *pangat*, a row, to eat food, cooked and served free by volunteers (sewadars).

These practices removed the inferiority complex of the poor and the so-called low caste persons. They started feeling equal to the other people. The sitting together, eating together, and living together as equals brought a social revolution in the region.

This was not to the liking of some of the high castes. Their leader known as Tapa, became jealous of the Guru and his teachings. His ego of being a high caste person, hence a superior human being, was hit by the social change introduced by the Guru. He started telling people, "Anyone who joins *pangat* and eats while sitting with low caste people will be polluted. He will lose his status as a high caste and will be considered a low grade soul. After his death, he will be sent to hell". The Guru, however, ignored all this and continued his mission of making all people feel equal. When the agents of Tapa started harassing and physically handling the visitors to the Gurdwara, Guru Amar Das decided to expose the true nature of this jealous man.

The Guru announced that any person who ate food in the *langar*, would be given a silver coin. Many high caste followers of Tapa left him and joined *pangat* to eat *Langar* sitting along with the poor and the so-called low castes. When the Guru raised the award to a gold coin, Tapa himself broke down. He got tempted to eat in *langar* for obtaining a valuable coin. However, he could not dare to sit in the same row with the persons whom he had been telling not to go there. Eating *langar* by Tapa would have meant going against his own beliefs that those who touch or sit with the low castes go to hell.

Tapa thought of a scheme to overcome his dilemma. He explained everything to his son, who was only a small boy. According to the plan, instead of guiding him through the main door, Tapa would drop his son over the back wall of the Gurdwara compound. The boy would join the *pangat*, eat *Langar* and claim a gold coin. He would pretend ignorance if somebody recognized him and questioned him about breaking the faith of his father.

Tapa took his son to the back of the Gurdwara, lifted him in his hands and dropped him over the wall of the compound. Instead of landing on his feet, the boy fell down in the yard and broke his leg. The floor of the compound was much deeper than assumed by Tapa.

Having been severely injured, the boy started crying aloud.

Hearing the cries of a child, some people came running to the spot to take care of the boy. When they asked the boy about his injury, he revealed the whole plan of his greedy father. He described them how Tapa dropped him over the wall and wanted him to get a gold coin by eating *Langar*. Everybody, who had gathered there, felt sorry for the unfortunate child. They laughed at Tapa and his plan to conceal his greedy nature.

The sad outcome of the jealousy of Tapa taught a great lesson to the people. The Guru recorded it in the Gurbani for future guidance to the people (Guru Granth pg. 315).

Having been badly exposed, Tapa could not face people with his head high. The incident was a moral death for him. Later, he suffered a miserable death, leaving a black spot of jealousy on his name.

SULHI KHAN and SULBHI KHAN

Guru Ram Das, the fourth Nanak, had three sons. The youngest Arjan Dev was very much committed to learning kirtan and reciting Gurbani. Of the three brothers, Prithi Chand was the eldest. He was assigned the responsibility of managing the affairs of the developing town, Amritsar, then known as Chak Ram Das. With this honorable position, instead of becoming a humble person, he was filled with ego. His behavior was not respectful or affectionate towards the disciples visiting Amritsar. Sometimes, he did not even listen to the Guru, his father.

Guru Ram Das before he expired, nominated Arjan Dev as his successor. Prithi Chand took ill of it. He became jealous of his brother and protested against it. He claimed that being the eldest son and being in charge of the development of the city, he deserves to be the Guru. He, therefore, asserted himself as Guru with the help of his associates and other Sikhs working with him for the management of the city. However, the Sikhs rejected his claims and did not show any love for him.

Prithi Chand was very much frustrated at his failure to dislodge Guru Arjan Dev. He created many obstacles to stop his younger brother from performing his responsibilities. His agents would misguide the visitors and obtain all the offerings from them, which they brought for the Guru. Within a short time, however, all the Sikhs knew that Prithi Chand was a pretender. Prithi Chand, having been rejected by the *sangat* left Amritsar and settled at Hehran, in

Lahore county. His wife belonged to that village.

The ego of Prithi Chand re-kindled his jealousy for his brother, Guru Arjan Dev. It motivated him to use force to remove his brother from Guruship or kill him. He worked out a plan to implement his decision. Prithi Chand went to Lahore, the capital of Punjab, to talk to the senior government officials. He told them that if they helped him get the Guruship, he would listen to them and cooperate with them. The administrator agreed with him. They deputed some army men to remove the Guru from Amritsar and install Prithi Chand there in his place. The army was permitted to use violence against the Guru, and even kill him if necessary to install Prithi Chand as Guru in Amritsar.

Prithi Chand was pleased with the success of his mission at Lahore. He wanted to please the commander Sulhi Khan assigned to help him to become the Guru. He requested Sulhi to pay a visit to his village. While showing him around his estate, Prithi Chand took him to a live brick-kiln. Clay bricks were being burnt for building a new temple which was to be managed by Prithi Chand to assert his claim of Guruship. Sulhi Khan was riding his horse. As soon as they reached the kiln, there was a sudden cracking noise. The horse got scared, went out of control, and jumped into the live kiln. Instantaneously, both the horse and the rider got burnt up leaving Prithi Chand stunned. All his hopes of becoming the Guru also got destroyed.

The wicked mind of Prithi Chand whipped him into making another attempt for the Guruship. He picked up courage to go to Lahore again. After some discussions, he again made the government agree to his request of helping him to become the Guru. Sulbhi Khan, the brother of Sulhi Khan was nominated as the commander of the force deputed to attack Amritsar.

The army reached near the city. When they were only a couple of miles away, they decided to rest there for the night. They wanted to make a plan for the next day to remove the Guru from the city. Prithi Chand imagined that he would be the Guru when the sun would shine on Amritsar the next day. However, God wished it differently.

Sulbhi Khan got angry with his servant that evening and severely rebuked him. The attendant was hurt very much but could do nothing. He knew that if he protested, Khan would have him killed. Therefore, he pretended that he regretted his omissions and would be careful in the future. The helpless fellow expressed no grudge and did not let his inner feelings be revealed to his master.

At midnight, when Sulbhi was sound asleep, the servant got up and picked up a wood-splitting ax. He raised it above his shoulders and swung it down with enough force to chop off the head of his commander. Leaving his master dead, he vanished away into the darkness of the night. A reference to the failure of the attacks made on the Guru is mentioned in the Guru Granth Sahib (pp. 371, 825).

The next morning the soldiers got ready to march to the city and waited for the orders of the commander. However, they did not observe any movement in the tent of Sulbhi Khan. When some soldiers went in, they were stunned to find the commander dead and his head lying on the ground.

The army returned and carried the coffin of their commander to Lahore. They cursed Prithi Chand. His jealousy resulted in another death.

WICKED BRAHMAN

Prithi Chand failed to dislodge the Guru but had one big consolation. He would think, ''Anyway the Guruship is going to come to my family because my brother Arjan Dev has no son.'' However one day, he received a big shock when he heard that a son, Har Gobind, was born to the Guru. Prithi decided to kill the innocent child. He made many attempts to achieve his objective, one such effort is mentioned below.

Prithi engaged a greedy Brahman and brought him around to kill the baby for a big reward. The plan was drawn to poison the baby. The Brahman would often go to the house of the Guru and fondle the baby. His visits were regular and the baby accepted him. The Brahman, while playing with the baby, would also feed him some yogurt. In this way, the Brahman won the confidence of the family and their near relatives.

One day, the Brahman brought poison with him to feed to the baby. As usual he got some yogurt from the house, secretly mixed poison in it, and offered it to the baby. The baby refused to eat it. When the Brahman tried to force yogurt into the mouth of the baby, he turned his face and started crying aloud. Every person around came running to know what went wrong with the child.

The Brahman was caught red handed. He was scared of the consequences. From his trembling hands the yogurt fell down on the floor. A dog standing nearby came fast and lapped it up very quickly. While the people were wondering why the baby was crying, the dog fell dead on the floor. The secret was revealed to everyone.

The Brahman had no alternative but to confess his crime and explain the involvement of Prithi Chand to the people gathered there. He felt extremely ashamed and regretted his heartless attempt to kill the baby. While he was narrating the plan to poison the baby, his conscious pricked him and he could not bear it. The wicked Brahman developed colic, which caused unbearable pain and he fell on the ground, wreathing in agony. Soon his soul departed leaving him dead before the eyes of many people. Regarding this incident, a brief reference is mentioned in the Guru Granth Sahib (pg. 1137).

This was such a mean and ghastly act on the part of Prithi Chand that people refused to talk to him. His jealousy resulted in the loss of two lives. He lost his face with the people. The Sikhs shunned the company of Prithi and his associates who were labeled Meenas (bad persons) by the people.

3

BABA BUDHA JI

Baba Budha Ji is recognized as one of the great Sikhs of the Guru period. He had the privilege of being blessed by the first six Gurus. He led an ideal Sikh life for more than a hundred years.

Baba Ji was born to Bhai Sugha in 1506 in village Kathu Nagal, district Amritsar. His parents named him Burha. He was only a child, when the family migrated to village Rumdas. Burha, being the son of a farmer, used to graze cattle like other boys of his age in the village. When Guru Nanak Dev Ji visited their village, he listened to the Guru preach.

Impressed by the sermons, one day he brought fresh milk for the Guru to have a chance to talk to the Guru directly. The Guru was pleased with his devotion. Bhai Burha Ji asked the Guru about the mission of human life and the way to achieve it. Guru Ji responded, "You are a young boy, but you are talking like a *Budha*, an experienced senior citizen." Since then, Bhai Burha became popular with his new name, Baba Budha Ji.

As advised by the Guru, Baba Ji adopted the life of a Sikh. He recited Gurbani, shared his earnings with the needy and wished well for everyone. People were much impressed by his lifestyle and devotion to service. Guru Ji also appreciated his living as an ideal Sikh.

Guru Nanak Dev Ji after his preaching tours to different countries in Asia, settled at village Kartarpur. Baba Ji would visit him to listen to the holy kirtan and the teachings of the Guru. One day, he was summoned by the Guru to Kartarpur for a special assignment. When Baba Budha Ji reached there, Guru Nanak told him to put a mark of respect on the forehead of Bhai Lehna Ji who was nominated as the successor to Guru Nanak.

Baba Budha Ji lived a long life of more than a hundred years. He was always called upon to perform this sacred assignment whenever the Guruship was passed on to the next successor. Baba Ji lived long enough to serve Guru Har Gobind, the sixth Nanak. Because of this honorable status, he was loved and respected very much by the Sikh masses.

When the work of digging the Amrit Sarovar was undertaken during the time of Guru Ram Das and continued through the Guruship of Guru Arjan Dev Ji, Baba Ji was nominated as the coordinator of the volunteers. There still stands a jujubee tree on the border of the Sarovar where Baba Ji sat while performing his responsibilities. After the completion of the construction work at Amritsar and the installation of the Sikh holy scripture, Baba Ji was honored as the first Granthi of the Harimandar Sahib.

After his sewa at Amritsar was over, Baba Budha Ji was given another important assignment at village Jhabal. A Sikh had offered Guru Ji a large piece of land in that village. The land was covered by trees and grazing lands. Milch animals and the horses of the Guru were kept there. Since Baba Ji was in charge and took care of the animals, the place became popular as Bir Baba Budha Ji. In memory of his services, a gurdwara now stands there with the same name.

Guru Arjan Dev Ji sent his son, Har Gobind, to that place and put him under the charge of Baba Ji. He was to teach the young boy to read and understand Gurbani, horse riding, wrestling, use of arms and other arts of defense.

Knowing that his body had become very weak and that death

was not very far away, Baba Ji requested the Guru to let him move to his own village of Rumdas. When he was about to die, Guru Har Gobind was there to bless him. Baba Ji died in 1631, at the mature age of 125 years. Baba Ji earned a permanent place in the minds of the Sikh community for his services to the Guru.

4

BHAI BIDHI CHAND

Bhai Bidhi Chand was born to Bhai Wasan, who lived at village Sur Singh. His mother belonged to Sarhali a famous village in Amritsar District. During his early days, Bhai Bidhi Chand got into the wrong company and became a dacoit. Bhai Adli, a Sikh since the days of Guru Ram Das, met him. Influenced by his good behavior, Bhai Bidhi Chand accompanied him to visit Amritsar. When he went before Guru Arjan Dev, he confessed openly that he was a dacoit by profession. The Guru advised him to earn his living honestly. His mind was changed there and then.

After the murder of Guru Arjan Dev, his son Guru Har Gobind put on two swords, representing *miri* and *piri*. This was a signal to the government that Sikhs would protect their human rights of worship if need be with the sword. Guru Har Gobind invited young men to come to Amritsar and learn the arts of self-defense and the use of arms. Bhai Bidhi Chand decided to volunteer his services to the Guru to teach the arts of war to the disciples.

Guru Har Gobind was arrested by the emperor of Delhi and imprisoned in the fort of Gwalior. Bhai Bidhi Chand went from village to village, informing people of the sacrifices made by the Gurus for the human rights of the weak. He, along with his *dhadi jatha*, would sing *vars* which brought *chardi kala* to the minds of the people. Later, when the Guru was released from the fort, Bhai Bidhi Chand became his body guard. He was appointed as the leader of one of the five divisions of the volunteer forces of the

Guru.

Bhai Bidhi Chand went to Lahore and met Meharban, the son of Prithi Chand, the elder brother of Guru Arjan Dev. He had started undesirable activities to undermine the image of the Guru and spread anti-Sikh rumors. When Bhai Sahib told him to give up his evil activities, Meharban was impressed by his advice. Afterwards, he did not dare to do anything against the Guru openly.

The rising image and strength of the Sikhs under the leadership of Guru Har Gobind was not to the liking of the governor of Lahore. He found an excuse to attack the Guru in May of 1629 with an army of 7,000 soldiers. Bhai Bidhi Chand played a significant role in fighting the army and defeating the government forces. He hit one of the commanders with his arrow and killed him. Mukhlis Khan, the other commander, was killed by the Guru himself.

A second battle was forced on the Guru when he was visiting Sri Hargobindpur. Bhai Sahib attacked one of the commanders with such force that he was routed and chased back to Lahore. This battle also ended in a victory for the Guru.

There is another famous incident related to the life of Bhai Bidhi Chand. Two highly valued thoroughbred horses of great quality were bought by the *sangat* of Kabul for the Guru. However, on the way to Amritsar, they were forcibly taken by the men of the governor when they were passing through Lahore. Bhai Bidhi Chand brought them back by a unique technique.

He dressed himself as a grass keeper and took a bundle of grass to the gate of the fort where the horses were kept under guard. He sold the grass to the caretaker at a very low price to make him his customer. In a couple of days they became friends and Bhai Bidhi Chand was given the job of bringing grass and feeding the horses. Bhai Bidhi Chand did this duty very devotedly and impressed all of the employees and the guards in the fort. Bhai Bidhi Chand made a plan to jump with a horse into the Ravi River which ran alongside the fort. At night, once in a while, he would throw a large boulder over the wall of the fort into the river. When the guards wanted to know the cause of the sound, he would say that there was a big animal in the river.

One day when he received his pay, he offered a big feast to the guards in the fort. When the guards were sound asleep at night, Bhai Bidhi Chand untied a horse, got on his back and jumped with it into the river. The guards came to know about it only when they got up in the morning. By that time, Bhai Bidhi Chand had already taken the horse to the Guru.

For bringing the second horse, Bhai Bidhi Chand went to Lahore again. He stayed with Bhai Bohru who told him that Sondhay Khan, the custodian of the horses was very worried about the loss of the horses. He was consulting astrologers to help him find the missing horse. Bhai Bidhi Chand dressed himself as an astrologer and got hold of other necessary gadgets used by astrologers. He went to the fort and sat in front of the gate.

He hinted to the caretaker of the horses to come to him because he could tell him who had taken the horses. Bhai Bidhi Chand immediately told the caretaker that the man who brought grass for the horses was the thief. This convinced the caretaker of the powers of the astrologer and he took him to Mr. Khan.

When he met Khan, Bhai Bidhi Chand explained to him the way in which the horse was stolen. Khan knew that everything Bhai Sahib was saying was correct. When he wanted to know the location of the stolen horse, Bhai Sahib said that he could tell that only at midnight by putting himself in the position from where the thief stole the horse. Khan came at midnight with his guards to find out about the horse. Bhai Sahib said that all of the guards should be inside doors and be sleeping on their beds as they were during the time of the theft. He told Mr. Khan that the thief had locked all of the guards and that he would do the same.

Addressing Mr. Khan, Bhai Sahib spoke, "Now I will tell you how and where the thief took the horse." He untied the horse, got on his back and said, "The thief got on the horse like this, jumped into the river and took the horse to Guru Har Gobind. I will also take this horse to the Guru to whom they belong." Before Khan could inform the guards, Bhai Sahib along with the horse had crossed the river. He then rode straight to the Guru.

Bhai Bidhi Chand was given another assignment to preach Gurmat to the people in Ayodhya. Sunder Shah, a Sikh and resident of that town, had requested Guru Har Gobind to send a preacher to that city. Guru Ji deputed Bhai Sahib for this important assignment.

Bidhi Chand was not only a brave and tactful soldier, but also a great devoted Sikh. While moving about and working, he always recited Gurbani. He prayed before undertaking any assignment. When he reached Ayodhya, he found that there were no Gurbani books for the people to read. When he was free from discussions, he started making copies of Gurbani hymns for the devotee Sikhs. Bhai Sahib did a lot of sewa there. He died in 1695.

The Guru converts bad people into holy soldiers and good preachers.

5

BHAI KALYANA

Bhai Kalyana was one of the few Sikhs who were assigned by Guru Arjan Dev Ji the great responsibility of going out to various places, educating people about Gurmat, and making collections for building Harimandar Sahib at Amritsar.

Bhai Sahib was sent to the hill areas of the Mandi state in the north of Punjab. Whenever he went there, he would associate some local people with him, discuss with them the principles of the Sikh faith and sing Gurbani kirtan to them. People looked forward to his visits because they loved to sit with him and listen to Gurbani recitations from him.

Once it was *Janam-Ashtmi* day, when Bhai Sahib was preaching Gurmat in the town of Mandi. The local ruler announced with the beat of a drum the significance of this Hindu religious day and ordered all people to keep fast on that day. In addition, people were required to worship Thakur, a special type of stone, on that day. This was a technique adopted by the Brahmans to collect money from the innocent people of the city.

Bhai Kalyana did not bother about it. He cooked his food as usual and shared it with local people. The matter was brought to the notice of the ruler, Hari Sain. He ordered Bhai Kalyana to appear before him and explain his position for disobeying the instructions of the ruler. In response, Bhai Sahib recited Gurbani quotations which meant that to please God, we should love and respect people instead of worshipping stones. Further, fasting has no religious value.

Hari Sain could give no arguments to challenge the statements of Bhai Ji, however, he observed, "I agree with you in principle, but you must be punished for disobeying my orders." Bhai Kalyana replied, "You have disrespected the wishes of God, who provides food for everyone to eat. Against this, you are instructing people not to eat food. Therefore, you are guilty of a bigger wrong by disobeying the mighty Lord who is the ruler of the whole world."

Hari Sain, who was suffering under the yolk of Brahmans and was practising meaningless rituals, was awakened. He decided to become a Sikh. He accompanied Bhai Kalyana Ji to Amritsar and got the blessings of Guru Arjan Dev.

Wherever we go, we must practise the Sikh faith and educate people about the greatness of the principles of the Sikh faith.

6

BHAI LANGAHA

The name of Bhai Langaha is mentioned among the famous Sikhs of the Guru period by Bhai Gurdas Ji in his *var* no. 11. He wrote "Chawdhari Langaha of the Dhillon clan lived in Patti and was a committed Sikh of the Gurus." Bhai Langaha lived in village Jhabal, about eight kilometers to the south of Amritsar. He was one of the three administrators of the Patti area yielding about 900,000 rupees of annual revenue to the government. He was the first person of the village to become a Sikh and helped other people to follow the faith.

Earlier, Bhai Langaha was a disciple of the Pir Sakhi Sarvar. This sect was a first step for Hindus to be converted to Islam. The followers of the Pir worshipped in the Pir-Khanna, a house of the Pir.

Guru Arjan Dev Ji built a Sikh center at Taran Taran and dug a sarovar there. A Sikh *sangat* was founded there to preach the faith among the people of this region who were attracted to the Pir. The Guru also opened a hospital for the handicapped and sick people. It was during these activities that Bhai Langaha came to know of the Sikh faith and met Guru Arjan Dev Ji. As a result of this, he replaced the Pir-Khanna in his house and established Sikh *sangat* there. The people would gather in the house to sing the virtues of the Lord. Bhai Langaha also donated a large parcel of land to the Guru for maintaining and grazing cattle and horses. This place was administrated by Baba Budha Ji and hence was named Bir Baba

Budha Ji.

When Guru Arjan Dev Ji was arrested and taken to Lahore, Bhai Langaha was one of the five Sikhs who went with the Guru to keep the Sikhs in touch with the conditions of the Guru. He did this at a great risk to himself for he could have been removed from his position or even arrested and murdered by the government for associating with the Guru.

After the execution of Guru Arjan Dev Ji, Bhai Langaha maintained his loyalty to Guru Har Gobind and remained a devoted Sikh.

When the governor of Lahore attacked Amritsar in 1629, it was the day of the marriage of Bibi Veero, the daughter of Guru Har Gobind. Knowing the impending attack on Amritsar by the army, the Guru sent his daughter and her mother to Bhai Langaha in village Jhabal for performing the marriage ceremony. Bhai Langaha did not hesitate to accept this responsibility knowing full well that it could result in repercussions by the government against him.

The family of Bhai Langaha remained committed to the Sikh faith after his death. His children and grandchildren associated with the Gurus and the Khalsa Panth. They took Amrit and joined the Khalsa Panth. They also provided food and other facilities for the Sikhs fighting guerrilla warfare during the early eighteenth century.

The *sakhi* of Mai Bhag Kaur, grandniece of Bhai Langaha is well known to the students of Sikh history. She organized the villagers to fight for Guru Gobind Singh when the Mughal army was pursuing him after he vacated Anandpur Sahib. She was able to collect a large number of Sikhs and intercept the army at Mukatsar where the Guru camped on the banks of a small lake. The Sikhs forced the army to retreat. Mai Bhag Kaur received many injuries and became unconscious. After treatment when she recovered, she remained with the Guru and accompanied him to the south. After the death of the Guru at Nanded, she continued to do sewa there. A gurdwara named after her was built near the Gurdwara Sach Khand at Nanded.

Another famous member of this family was Sardar Baghail Singh, who was the head of the Kror Singhia Misl. He was not only a brave soldier but also a great statesman. He took over Delhi and built gurdwaras at the places connected with Guru Tegh Bahadur and Guru Har Krishan Ji. He performed this service before the end of the eighteenth century.

Sardar Khazan Singh, who was also a member of this family, did great service to the Panth during the period of Maharaja Ranjit Singh. Sardar Karam Singh, a great historian of the early twentieth century, also belonged to this family.

The devotion and commitment of Bhai Langaha helped his generations to feel pride in being Sikhs, living as Sikhs and dying as Sikhs.